The Anthology
of
Magical Poetry
Volume I

Cleveland K. Kincade

Kincade Publishing Company

Copyright © 2010
Cleveland K. Kincade
All rights reserved

Written in the United States of America

Library of Congress
Control Number-1-723-472
ISBN -13: 978-0615580647
ISBN - 10 : 0615580645

First Printing (1,000 copies)

Kincade Publishing Company
K. Kincade
P.O. Box 635
San Luis Rey, CA 92068

Poet's Notes

Reader,

As you read this material you are making my hopes and dreams come true! I would like to take this opportunity to thank you for allowing me to do so. I am hopeful that my magical poetry will capture your poetic heart and soul, for the journey I have experienced in my life to deliver my magical poetry to you and the world has presented many obstacles. Without your support they would have been insurmountable.

The poems I have composed are inspirited with emotion, clarity, and compassion. They are designed to acquaint you with the poetic creations of my world, expressed into words from deep within. I hope my magical poetry will eventually take me to where my poetic soul is destined to be and to achieve what I was sent here to achieve, all in one lifetime. My ambition continues to drive me as I hope to remain a symbol of inspiration to poetry lovers across the globe, reminding people that love is the strongest entity of all. Adversity, trials, and tribulations can unfortunately lock our body, but never can they trap our mind. Magical poetry keeps the spirit alive, and is the voice of love, and life in ever flowing motion.

Thank You

Cleveland K. Kincade

Dedication

I dedicate this poem book in loving memory of my grandfather Cleveland Kincade, and my grandmother Elnora Kincade. The creation I am today is a replica and reflection of you. I carry your spirit with me all of my days in life here on Earth. The creator's thoughts, my heart, and your soul, now live hand-in-hand. Thank you!

Acknowledgements

I would first like to thank and give all my praises, honor, and glory to the almighty omnipotent one, my true energy of eternal love and life. Righteousness and prosperity are the key. I thought I knew the power and value of your love, then I found you in me. You have uplifted my soul and anointed my spirit with your existence. I thank you for making me into the creation I am and will always be. I pray that you will continue to amplify the entity of my heart so I can represent life here on earth as your spiritual instrument of hope, knowledge, insight, and wisdom. The ambition of my existence 1 realize now is to reach the tabernacle of the mountain top.

To my beautiful wife and soul mate Kalia, my true clairvoyance of beauty—ambitious, courageous, loyal, and sublime. Your very existence has been the edification of my emotional and spiritual purification. Your dedication, guidance, patience, assistance, and life time support have made this magical poetry book and project a living reality. Is this what the momentum of love feels like? If so, then you are truly something magical and amazing. Through your almond eyes not only do I see through the windows to your soul, but I see everything that I have ever needed, wanted, and desired within you. My love for you is immeasurable and infinite, you are my rock.

To my daughter Knijah-Ayana, the most beautiful image of myself there could ever be. You are a special child, my first born, a leader, full of energy, shinning like the night star. You are my angel, and daddy loves you. I will hold your hand until you reach your destination in life. You are a wonderful spirit, my little diva and a majestic flower, Ayana. Through you I will achieve eternal life. My love for you is ever flowing and I thank you with all my heart and soul. You are not alone.

To my son Cleveland-Kanye, Mr. Unbreakable, who has the sense of a wise man, and possess the heart of a god-filled child. My little big guy, what joy you have brought to my life, the greatest reinvention of myself, supreme and pre-eminent. Your perfect just how the creator made you, always remember who you are and be yourself. Allow the voices of consciousness and divine truth to be your guide in life. Know that you were sent here to make the impossible, possible. I love you son.

To my special Rose, my mother whose love exemplifies the beauty of a rose garden. You have always inspired me and motivated me to keep the faith no matter how hard life got. I love you Rosa, the bouquet of roses is for you. Thanks for loving me, that's where life started for me.

To my brothers, I love each and every one of you the same—Ernest, Brian, Patrick, Daniel, and Vernon. When were together we were a force to be reckoned with. The unification of brotherhood is for y'all, man. Stay strong, remain wise, and keep your focus. Dreams do come true. I love you guys.

Donna, thank you for always being there for me when I needed you. You're a beautiful spirit whose advice and words of wisdom have brought joy to my life. I appreciate the strength that you have provided to me and my family. You will always be mom's nana. Thank you.

To my nephews Isaiah and Elijah, niece Elyssa, cousins Shadell, Kia, Mya, Michael, Kim, Dolores, Elnora, Remal, Calvin, Vasser, Auntie Martha, and to all those who have been a positive motivating force in my life. Ernest H, Earnest C, Sharon, Jimmy, Bre, Kim, Aunt Bill, Robert K, Lisa, Debra, Dajuan, Anthony VV, Basheer A, Clela, Norman Y, Andre J, Vernon SR, Jermaine VV, Hola-Ray, Tony, Jason, Michael W, Deajanee, Teajanne, Tony, Tracy, Mr. Patterson, Uncle Artist, Lelani, Quasy, Reese, Ester, Solo, Kijah, Charles, Tony, Red, Daun.

And to all those who contributed to my vision and dream: Steve C and Lincoln B, your artwork remains a pillar of positive energy and a statement of poetic magic and design. Nobody makes it anywhere without a great team.

May life's magical poetry keep healing lives, touching hearts and souls, mending relationships, and spreading love and hope to society.

This gift was given to me so that I can do something positive for the people in my life, and for the people of the world. Thank you all for your love and support. Nothing comes without hard work and struggle.

Magical poetry keeps the spirit alive, and is the voice of love and life in ever-flowing motion.

Cleveland K. Kincade
A Poetic Soul

My words were written.
They were inscribed in a book.
Job 19:23

They were engraved on a rock,
with an iron pen and led forever.
Job 19:24

Ecclesiastes 4:14

Special Thanks

Maya Angelou, Amiri Baraka, Desiree A. Barnwell (Mrs.Lawrence S. Cumberbatch), Arna Bontemps, Denise Sanders Brooks, Gwendolvn Brooks, Charlotte Brown, Margaret Burroughs, Phyllis Bynum, John Henrik Clarke, Lucille Clifton, Charlie Cobb, Hardv Crosslin, Paul Laurence Dunbar, Suliuman El Hadi, James Emanuel, Mari E. Evans, Nikki Giovanni, Robert E. Hayden, Frank Horne, Langston Hughes, Ja Jahannes, Georgia Douglas Johnson, James Weldon Johnson, Layding Kaliba, Doc Long, Naomi Long Madgett, Haki Madhubuti, Barbara Mahone, Pauli Murray, Gordon Nelson, Adiodun Oyewole, Jean Parrish, Comrad Kent Rivers, Sonia Sanchez, Gil Scott-Heron, Ntozake Shange, Joyce Carol Thomas, Alice Walker, and Margaret Abigail Walker.

This special thanks is for the poets who paved the way before me. Your legacy lives on.

Thank you,

Cleveland K. Kincade
A Poetic Soul

Preface

This book of magical poetry was written from the heart and soul, composed for you, the society of today and the people of tomorrow. Designed to help you appreciate the joy and spiritual poetic messages that poetry has to offer. It also brings a poetic eclipse to the rhythmic sounds and sights of nature, and life itself. I hope that it will capture the spirit of a broad array of readers and poetry lovers across the world.

While magical poetry unravels with the wisdom of time, you'll recognize the unique legendary elements of this world which revolves amongst our atmosphere and our intimate souls, each and every passing day. The Anthology of Magical Poetry, Volume I will take you beyond the past, into the present, and allow you to foresee into the future with the power of poetry. The poems are rich in literary word swagger and poetic theme. You will also become more acquainted with the author and his poetic spirit. As his relentless effort and struggle presents a door way to deliver his poetic justice to you the reader.

The emotions and feelings expressed in these poems are meant to be extremely moving. They are created to relate to you and make you a part of the poetic creations of the world. To open eyes, expand minds, and touch hearts. The poems are arranged in order of past, present, and future events experienced from the soul and spirit of the author's ever-existing design.

May the magic of this poetry book and the words inspirited within the poems be a tool of enlightenment to captivate the awareness of your spiritual being and entity, and to justify the fact that no obstacle is insurmountable, and no stumbling block is unmovable. This poetic justice is my form of clarity: *The Anthology of Magical Poetry Volume I.*

Enjoy.

Introduction

This novel came to me in a vision, which allowed me to express and share with you, the reader, my deepest and most intricate thoughts from memory. I then formulated my inner feelings and life experiences into my magical poetry. As I journey through life as the molded symbol of a poetic soul, my poems are inspirited in this anthology, as an exodus for the people. My ambition and mission is to fulfill my purpose in life, and what I was created and meant to be. So I offer the world my fully enlightened and stimulating product from a new-millennium poet, with a poetic soul, *The Anthology of Magical Poetry Volume I.*

Now that I have seen in life what life has wanted me to see, and attained spiritual virtue within the circumference of my entity, the road of my physical voyage toward spreading the joy of love and my magical poetry across the globe will eventually take me to where I was destined to be, and to achieve what I was sent here to accomplish all in one lifetime.

Thus my desire in life to see the beauty in growing old, and to know that I have created a legacy and dynasty with my magical poetry. The struggle, hard work, and perseverance I have experienced to consume insight, knowledge, and wisdom are the key elements to my existence and will live forever through my seeds, deeds, and poems, and those who loved me, and those whom I love unconditionally.

I would also like for my poems and this magical poetry book to be read, felt, and to touch people across the world. And whatever the message may be that I've been sent here to deliver and share with you today or tomorrow. Let it first capture the world's ear, then captivate the globe's heart. As I aspire in life to be the first spirit in my life's story, to achieve and create something positive and prosperous by my own spiritual image and design. Reminding people, by way of my poems, and magical poetry, that love is a far more stronger entity than hate.

In closing, I would like to thank the creator for blessing me with the spiritual gift to express my talent and poetic soul in this poem book, and the life's experiences to share in my poetry with the world. This poetic novel is my lifeline to the globe, and my voice to speak magical poetry to the people of the world. The poetic soul is alive, along with magical poetry.

Adversity can sometimes lock your body, but never can it trap your mind. Magical poetry keeps the spirit alive and is the voice of love and, life in ever-flowing motion!

Table of Contents

Chapter 1   A Poetic Soul

I Am 2
My Creation Runs Free 3
Free 4
The Creation I Am 5
Transformed 6
Poetic Soul 7
Air 8
There Lives a Place 9
Thought 10
It Comes From 11

Chapter 2   Love

Love 13
The Momentum of Love 14
Love Knows 15
The Pinnacle of Love 16
The Symmetry of Love 17
When Love Changes 18
The Love I Possess 19
The Footsteps of Love 21
Loves Mercenary 22
Love Speaks 23

Chapter 3   Peace

Peace 25
The Antidote of Tranquility 26
Clouds 27
What If 28
Tranquil...29
Once Before 30
Fulfillment 31

Serenity's Eye..32
Serene...33
The Recipe 34

Chapter 4   Beauty
Beauty 36
The Clairvoyance of Beauty 37
Beauty and I..38
Beauty's Garden 39
Beauty from Up Above....................................40
Admire 41
Beauty and Grace...42
Almond Eyes...43
First Place...44
Together We Stand 45

Chapter 5   Infinity
Infinity..47
The Axis of Infinity 48
Immortal...49
Wind...50
Limitless and Free...51
Marriage 52
Vows I...53
Vows 11 54
Vows 111 55
Love Walks with Me..56

Chapter 6   Perseverance
Perseverance 58
The Mountain Top 59
Images..60
Ever Flowing...61
Future 62
Significant 63

Bells 64
Shooting Star...65
Sacred Garden..66
Mountains 67

Chapter 7   Pain
Pain 69
The Pendulum of Pain...70
Tears...71
Empty Hearts 72
Darkness..73
The Dynamics of Pain...74
A Silent Cry 75
Rain Drops 76
The Tears of a Shadow 77
The Things I've Lost 78

Chapter 8   Struggle
Struggle...80
The Dynamics of Struggle 81
Sunset to Sunrise...82
The Sycamore Tree...83
Another Cold Morning..84
Alpines Home 85
Pathway..86
Our Time...87
The Magnitude of Isolation.................................88
Never Ending Freeway 89

Chapter 9   Destiny
Destiny..91
The Seasons of Destiny.......................................92
Celestial Race 93
Horizon 94
Destination 95

Foreseen 96
Home..97
Hypnotized..98
Y.O.U...99
The Petals of My Flower 100

Chapter 10   Prosperity
Prosperity...102
The Dreams of Prosperity 103
Dreams 104
Picnic..405
Mirage 106
Reasons 107
The Authenticity Within 108
First Degree..109
Before It's Too Late 110
Commitment 111

Chapter 11   Romance
Romance 113
The Vibrations of Romance...........................114
Fireplace...115
When Passion Pursues Immunity..................116
Where I Wanna Be..117
Chemistry...118
A Gift 119
Taken..120
Vibrations...121
Recapture and Recreate 122

Chapter 12   Eternity
Eternity...124
The Seeds of Eternity...................................125
Majestic Flower 126
Unbreakable 127

Forever 128
A Young Heart..129
Goodbye...130
Jewels...131
Night Star...132
Bouquet of Roses 133

Chapter 13   Loneliness
Loneliness 135
The Chills of Loneliness 136
Chills..137
Without You 138
Abandoned 139
With You...140
The Entity of the Heart 141
The Kiss 142
Echoes..143
Broken...144

Chapter 14   Balance
Balance...146
The Scales of Balance.............................147
Today 148
Un-Movable 149
Melody 150
Kinetic Souls Entwine 151
Amazing..152
The Way..153
Umbrella 154
Rock..155

Chapter 15   Clarity
Clarity 157
The Tabernacle of Clarity 158
Last Request..159

Truth..160
Windows to the Soul.....................................161
Karma...162
How I Feel for You 163
Moments 164
Flow 165
One Day 166

Chapter 16   Change
Change 168
The Transition of Change 169
Transition 170
Tomorrow 171
Listen..172
Lost Innocence 173
Visions 174
Street Light...175
The Yard 176
Ready 177

Chapter 17   Existence
Existence..179
The Ambition of Existence 180
Rose Garden...181
Ambition 182
The Unification of Brotherhood....................183
People..184
People Everywhere 185
I Am People 186
The Unseen 187
Silent Thoughts..188

Chapter 18   Life
Life..190
Life's Perception 191

Life Changes 192
Light...193
This Place..194
The Sea 195
The Past..196
Life's Expedition..197
Life's Abyss 198
Life's Cycle 199

Chapter 19   Time
Time..201
The Triangle of Time......................................202
Guess...203
Away..204
Present...205
Past...206
To Reach You 207
Time and Time Again......................................208
In Peace...209
Soaring Through Time.....................................210

Chapter 20   Nature
Nature's Wind..212
Thanks to You..213
Gentle Winds 214
The Eye Watches 215
Pine Tree 216
Up Above..217
Seasons...218
The Eye 219
Oasis...220
The Prayer..221

Chapter 21   Magical Poetry

Magical Poetry 223
Poetic Magic 224
Reflections 225
Dreamer..226
Yesterday 227
Magical Potion...228
Presence 229
There Could Be 230
The Orchard of Light 231
The Never Ending Story 232

Cleveland Kincade

The Ever-Flowing Beginning

Chapter 1

A Poetic Soul

Magical poetry is the voice of life in spirit and shared with you the world from my poetic soul. It has kept my spirit alive and has allowed me to experience the many wonderful creations of this world all in one lifetime. With this special gift I hope to spread the power of love, joy, and happiness to all who seek the truth in the midst of darkness, and to all who understand that the light lies within the depths of our infinite souls.

Thus my journey continues on, as I remain currently in the physical form, and expire slowly, as a symbol of hope and inspiration to all those who believed in me and my magical poetry, never forgetting that love is a far more stronger entity than hate, and hopes and dreams do come true, all you have to do is believe in the soul within you.

Magical poetry keeps the spirit alive, and is the voice of life in ever-flowing motion.

I Am

I am
My poetic soul's creation,
An infinite spirit.

The most precious gift in life, is when
You reach a point in your life, when
You realize who you are, what your
Mission and purpose in life is, and the
Reason for being, the creation I am,
And will always be.

My Creation Runs Free

In a race for the heavens, I start from the
Earth, my finish poetic, a pupil of holistic
Quintessence, the essence of a prince, a true
King, traveling, moving across the oceans seas,
The souls of my ancestors make up my
Genealogy, three-hundred-and-sixty degrees,
By sheer design, my movements, are of the
Omnipotent one, the mission, a spiritual dream
In time, inspirited in history, artistic, creative
Hieroglyphics, once a pharaoh reborn,
Journeying through the present, eternal into
The future, blood of historic tradition flows
Through my veins,
like the waves of the Red Sea,
The Nile River, sickled, my cells in
Astrological history, composed in the sky,
Solomon, embedded in the revelation of my
Legacy, genesis, exodus, the chains are worn
Internally, but my creation runs free.

Free

Free, as is the spirit that lives free,
Freedom lives within me,
I am free.

The Creation I Am

The eye, in I, lives alive, an embodied spirit
Mineralized, thy spiritual visions, solar
Energized, I stand before you, in the present
Dignified, a Libra of air and sapphire,
Materialized, our footprints in the burning
Sand, he walks with me hand in hand, solidified,
Genes of a confident soul, virtue of the mind
Guided by hope and faith, with the will of a
Bronze statue, I shall prosper as a legend,
Legendary, my ambition in place the creation I
Am is the creation I will always be.....

Transformed

A transformed spirit, searching,
Deep from within frosted windows,
Lighting truth.

Poetic Soul

The thesis and theory of a poetic soul, the
Creation I am, scientifically speaking, a
Prophecy, the heavens shall give way to the
Spirit, a new breath of life and truth I breathe,
A new language whispered, my poetic soul's
Destiny, to spread thy wings to the sun, the
Creation I am, the last testament, his beloved
Son.

Air

A breath of life,
Silently moving endlessly,
Essence ever flowing.

There Lives a Place

There lives a place where clairvoyance
Embraces nature's articulate creativity,
Then embodies mysticism, into the depth of
Love and spirit within thee, there lives a
Place, a distant but near place, where love,
Loves with no limit, presents no beginning
Vast, no future ending, nor past in this
Place of pure splendor, ambition, and
Passion exists everywhere, where the sun
Conveys poetic life to the horizon, rising
Then setting, as destiny encompasses with
Gnostics, it travels over the surfaces of
Land, and sea, there lives a place, a distant
But near place within thee, where ever
After allows thy spirit to run free, and
Then becomes captured, for the love that
Engages thou and thee, lives in refuge, and
Harmony, while residing amongst the
Drifting winds, as freedom of spirit and
Love travel freely with no end, there
Lives a place, a distant but near place
Within thee.

Thought

An illuminating light,
A solidified vision,
Mind's creation.

It Comes From

It comes from, listening to the voices within,
It comes from, seeing the light in the darkness,
Respecting life's elements and nature's
Dominion, it comes from, believing, having
Faith, and allowing the soul to travel in peace
Freely, it comes from, revelations, and visions
Of silence in its entirety, it comes from, the
Relaxation deep within the spirit, it comes
From, elevation mentally, physical
Perseverance, it comes from, knowledge,
Wisdom, and simple gifts of love and virtue,
It comes from, up above to deep in the soul, it
Comes from, the entity in which you are, thus
Always remember where it comes from,
Because it comes from, the light that shines
Through and through, and that light that glows,
It comes from you.

Chapter 2

Love

The greatest force of all, is being
Possessed by the sheer endearment of divine
Love, impelled within the depth of our souls
Being, passionately driven, vehemently
Journeying, in ever-flowing motion,
Through time and space.
The momentum of love's magnitude also
Transcends the mind, heart, body, and soul by
Its amiable tenderness, its power, its shining
Attraction and emotional compassion.
The momentum of love evolves in a
Realm of all that love is, and all that love
Was created to be.

Love

Ever-flowing intimate souls,
Traveling endless horizons,
Nature's soul mates.

The Momentum of Love

A subtle knock, love's door bell rings, the
Momentum of love, two souls arriving
Infinitely, as the wind blows illuminating the
Trees, designed our footsteps, sublime our
Entities, flowing in the breeze, equal with
Love's trinity, two hearts beating as one, now
Faithfully entering, blessed into the kingdom
Of love eternally, our souls slowly, visiting
Momentum's virtual reality, this eclipse,
Handed to us, the distinctive sound of nature,
Opens the gates, the secret trust, joy and fear
Loves integrity, divinely framed amongst a
Sacred spiritual time portal, two
Distinguished spirits speak enchanting
Thoughts immortal, the momentum of love,
The immortality of two souls, the final
Delivery of clarity, virtuous instruments of
Love equipped luxuriously, architecturally
Intertwined, two intricate exhilarating minds,
Magnificently intriguing, the momentum of
Love, two lifelines crossing, celestial bodies,
Infatuated, love marinated, saturated beings,
The momentum of love, the prognosis of
Ecstasy.

Love Knows

Love knows, that dreams of love do come
True, love knows, only of love's devotion,
Loyalty, that loves absolute, while love
Knows, not of love with no limit, love possesses
Only love, that loves with divine endearment,
Love knows, that within love, love lives
Infinite, love knows, only of patience and
Understanding, why? Because love is joy and
Love is pain that over stands love's
Relationships, you see, love possesses an entity
Of its own, while love is standing strong, next
To the one you love, all in the name of love,
Love knows, autumn, summer, winter, and fall,
For love knows, that love conquers all, love
Knows, that as love continues to flourish, and
Grow, thoughts of love adjoins hearts, and
Souls, love knows, only of purity, living within
The spirit of love faithfully, receiving love as
Love shares love unconditionally, love knows,
Hope and faith, destiny and fate, love knows,
Karma with love's forgiveness, true love with
Balance, and essence, love knows, the beauty in
Joy and happiness, careful yet bold, the only
Vows love knows, is the love that lives within,
That love knows.

The Pinnacle of Love

The pinnacle of love moves freely amongst
The realm of life, flying a flight, like an eagle
With spread wings throughout the skies,
Soaring into a burst of flames, as one, igniting
Love's eternal fire, the elite pinnacle of our
Soul's intimate desires, by a watchful eye,
Acute are the lights upon watch towers,
Reflecting radiance and ambiance within our
Soul's unmovable heart, in the midst of
Crashing tides, against the rocks of infinite
Oceans, summits the essence of nature's life
Calling the pinnacle of love in poetic motion,
And tranquil devotion.

The Symmetry of Love

Is our love, the foundation of eternity,
Shared like wild horses galloping, racing
Across the earth's fertile land into infinity?
Is our love, the symbol of truth and
Perseverance overcoming, is our love,
Obstacles with just our hearts and spirits
Still standing, is our love, priceless, like a
Diamond and pearl both essential jewels of
Life in the rough evolving, awakened, what is
Our love in this limitless world of time, and
Motion? Is our love, a murmur in the wind, or
The spiritual essence of past, future and
Present, is our love, the chemistry, and
Symmetry of the moon, and stars within the
Immense sky, is our love, sunshine, connected
as one divine, is our love, inspirited in the
Constellations above, what is our love? Destiny
Viewed in the eyes of reality, or is our love, a
Mirror's reflection of monotony, seen threw
The windows of our soul, that meant to be
Moment love met, till the never ending
Moment love grows old, what is our love? A
Flickering reflection of remembrance, and
Compassion, or is our love, a love story based
On illusion and deception, what is our love?

When Love Changes

When love changes, a calm subtle breeze of
Wind slowly, crystallizes into a puddle of
Tear drops, when love changes, soaking into a
Concrete pond, splashing thy heart amongst
The pouring rain, when love changes, poetry in
Motion becomes love's silent darkness, the
Umbrella of thy love and life, complacent of
Sunny days, once comforted by the blossoming
Flowers, balancing earth, and energy at
Sunrise, when love changes, in the light of a
Still morning, thy soul shall answer
Compassionately, wholeheartedly, striving as
One to weather the storm, as love's mystical
Vintage portrait conveys way, perpetual bliss,
Grasping the synchronicity of symmetry's
Spirit, when love changes, the clouds become
Grey, when love changes, our chemistry no
Longer reflects the symbol of eternity, love's
Sacred element, calmly evolving the
Sensitivity of your emotions, a silhouette of
Your presence, the sunsets, when love changes,
Under the moonlit skies, ambition's entrance
Where are you roaming, thy soul mate heaven
Sent, our seeds planted, watered in the soil of
Marriage, vows no longer in the middle of
Love's birth and death, when love changes,
Life's fearless spirit, what distant realm has
Thy love drifted to, when love changes fairy
Tales become untrue, when love changes.

The Love I Possess

The love I possess is for you, it is as strong as
Such, that the glorious sound of love's
Unbreakable winds explore graciously within
Every corner of thy heart and soul, the
Golden path of our unmovable love continues,
As we flourish with affection as one, together
Holding on close, in our hand, and heart love's
Burning torch carrying away the illuminating
Clouds of storms, then with tears of joy, and
Emotion flooding the earth, quiet and still,
While faith exiles fear, a subtle soft kiss of
Reassurance, furnishes intensely, your love's
Signature, symmetry, inspirited, on velvet
Leaves of tapestry, the love I possess is for
You, a mortal fairytale of invitation, and pure
Splendor, paved in harmony, painted with
Grace, passion's portrait, entwined by thought,
Ruling thy heart, wearing a crown of
Celebration, the veil placed upon a silent vow,
The essence of life's magical poetry, our love
Written in stone, transcending amongst the
Stars, the love I possess is for you, and is as
Such forever strong, unmovable allowing
Heaven, to gravitate our love ever closer,
Rather far or near, divine the love I possess is
For you, thy sun shines in this domain bright,
Unconquered in love's vast world, as karma
Burns, transporting paradise to everlasting
Fire and air, engulfing love's innocence with

Nature's bliss, where time is kinetic and told by
The infinite tides, crashing upon the glittering
Sand at moments, a sanctuary of eternal love,
Passion willingly entangled in bondage, under
The sun and moon, the love I possess is for you,
Symbolizing our love's journey unmoved, the
Love I possess is for you.

The Footsteps of Love

Rose petals and violets embrace with a
Soulful kiss, as they lie deeply rooted into
The earth's sacred garden of love, the stems
Of soil and life as one grow passionately,
Imprinting the footsteps of love, planted
Deeply upon the sand symbolizing the essence
Of love's celestial entities, the breeze of wind
Spiritually blowing amongst the petals with
Affection and quintessence, love's perfect
Preservative, flowing throughout the
Atmosphere an aroma of candles scented,
Burning crisply, as the cracked windowpane
Rests in the still of immortal darkness,
Striving to deliver light, felicity composed in
Thy heart, the footsteps of love the
Reflection of light in the dark, the footsteps
Of love.

Love's Mercenary

A solemn morning arises, limitless, evermore
Endless, capturing love's acute eyes through a
Window, keenly gazing infinitely into the
Sunrise, clairvoyance setting over the
Horizon, calmly, leaving its imprint upon the
Heart and soul, love's mercenary, two entities
Entwined as one, awakening then mounting
Swiftly into eternity, with loving gallantry,
Nature's soul mates, love's mercenary, chasing
Life indefinitely, as the moon leads and the
Stars follow, autumn's fragrance, a heartfelt
Welcoming, thy sight resting upon the colors
Of the sky, love's purest image of bliss and
Divinity, speechless, love's mercenary,
Connoisseurs of devotions ecstasy, connected
Cosmically, heaven's treasures, of eternal
Passion and sublime celerity, the reason we
Live as one, for love as love's mercenaries.

Love Speaks

When love speaks, it speaks to the heart and
Soul, and with every whisper of every moment
Experienced, when love speaks, the heart shall
Beat like the peak of a mountains waterfall,
Touching the emotions, and feelings, allowing
Nothing to feel greater than when love calls,
Just listen to the heart and soul, when love
Speaks it speaks many languages all from the
Heart of your soul.

Chapter 3

Peace

One's desire for peace lies elevated in
Grasp, upon a realm of exclusive remedy.
A tranquil thought, freedom of spirit,
Which gives way defining and exemplifying,
The antidote of tranquility .

Peace

A tranquil realm,
Freedom of spirit,
Infinite solitude.

The Antidote of Tranquility

Upon the horizon lies a realm of peace and
Tranquility, thus my spirit sets on a never
Ending journey towards this destiny,
Protected by a warm blanket of love and
Comfort from the sun and moon, as my
Spiritual vessel continues to travel, eluding
Evil, but awakened by truth and reality, the
Mechanics of this affirmation of tranquility
That flows within the molded entity of my
Soul, I grasp tightly, knowing that my ending
Will be shaped by my beginning, all which
Evolves in the same environment, in which I
Search for peace, and resolution in the
Antidote of tranquility.

Clouds

An angel's resting place,
Far beyond ones dreams,
Pillow of love.

What If

What if, our souls could run free, where
Would they go? What if, color evolved only in
The rainbow and freedom was only a mere
Companion and soul mate of struggle? What if,
Your hopes and dreams were simply just you
Believing and faith within happiness could
Never be tainted by humility? What if, courage
Could outweigh pride and love was two doves
Flying together as you and I? What if, we were
Truly made up of the stars, would the
Constellations be our companions and lifetime
Guide? What if?

Tranquil

The peace that lives in spirit,
The peace that evolves in the soul,
Finally at peace.

Once Before

Once before, these feelings and thoughts I
Believe I have experienced many times once
Before, could I have been a poet, perhaps the
Composer of magical poetry once before,
Could I have been a prince then a king, ever
Flowing once before, could my soul have
Traveled many decades in time through the seeds
Of past, present, and future generations once
Before, could I have possibly been a tourist of
Life and death, each day expiring amongst
Space and time, once before, could I have found
Myself, within myself once before, could I
Have finally seen the eye, in I, once before,
Could I have been a messenger with a spiritual
Message to deliver to the world once before,
Could I have been an inspirational and
Motivational voice of clarity and truth, that
Spoke reality and peace to the youth, could I
Have been an eagle flying and soaring with
Spread wings across the infinite ocean seas,
Could I have been a lion in the jungle or a
Panther traveling across land and the earth's
Soil once before, could my life have already
Been written once before, could I have been a
Falling star sent from up above once before,
These feelings and thoughts I believe I have
Experienced many times, once before.

Fulfillment

Satisfied beyond compare,
Complete happiness,
Devote love.

Serenity's Eye

My thoughts travel like a message in an
Hourglass bottle, with every experience of
Every minute rippling amongst the waves of
The ocean's seas, as the sight of serenity's eye is
Placed upon me, firewood burns crisply upon a
Distant island, where tranquility and serenity
Lies, my spirit enjoys the sounds and melodies
That the birds sing, as a choir of butterflies
Fly freely, traveling the earth in sequences
My soul remains hypnotized and intertwined in
Divine order, then the sun rays shine bright,
Reviving my soul like the morning sunlight
Escaping from the midst of darkness, this
Splendor of nature's artwork, allows my
Arrival upon this distant island to only be
Seen in the captive eye of serenity.

Serene

Romance travels freely,
Emotions bridge feelings,
Serene awakening.

Recipe

The recipe of a skillful soul, magical
Poetry, brass and eternal, a relic statue,
Cultivated, as youth expires, mixing the
Ingredient of struggle, obstacles perceived
And consumed with intricate thoughts, still
Vigorous and joyful, this great gift, the recipe
Of fearless knowledge, shaken as the world
Turns, like the leaves on the trees, wisdom
Handed down, in honor of survival to
Persevere with destiny, danger evolves every
Where, but insight of this opposite cause allows
The pour of heart and courage from life's
Hourglass, to view reality, the mission, the
Impossible, the goal, the possible, the recipe of
A skillful soul, magical poetry, keeps the
Spirit alive and ever flowing, until the recipe
Is complete, and life is no longer served cold,
And I no longer incomplete, the recipe.

Chapter 4

Beauty

Love's impact upon the heart and soul can
Only be defined as the clairvoyance of
Beauty and the clairvoyance of beauty is
She.

Beauty

A majestic ambiance,
Of divine essence,
Beauty's clairvoyance.

The Clairvoyance of Beauty

If beauty was time she would be, the
Clairvoyance of cosmic infinity, love's
Instrument of passion, traveling, on a
Pendulum of love at life's speed, like a
Shooting star across the midnight sea, the
Clairvoyance of beauty, has been written in
The skies constellation you see, beauty is
Eternally free, spiritually healing, the
Clairvoyance of beauty is she, forever
Floating like a diamond, amongst the rough
Shores of a rivers stream, reflecting the
Clairvoyance of life's beauty, while thy heart
Soaks in loves seductive aura of eternal
Intimacy, majestic, divine, and supreme, the
Clairvoyance of beauty is she.

Beauty and I

Thy eyes rest mesmerized by the sight of
Beauties angelic chemistry, a poetic story
Intertwined in a realm of reality, with a
Magical destination, beauty and I, mystically
Hypnotized, as one inclined spiritually, as the
Reflection of beauty's truth shines through and
Through, ever flowing while love runneth over,
Two lifelines cross, and intimate powers are
Revealed unto thee, alluring slowly, and
Penetrating mentally, a deep state of love and
Tranquility surface, emotions captivated and
Divine, as thy eyes rest mesmerized by the sight
Of beauty's angelic chemistry, I shall become
The shining light of thy heart's ecstasy
Eternally, beauty and I, the foundation of
Love's journey, unmoved and forever meant to
Be beauty and I.

Beauty's Garden

Beauty, I have finally found in you, inner
Strength of a majestic flower, connected to
The spirit within thy soul, blooming, and
Blossoming throughout thy life, summer, fall,
Winter, spring, our reasons, four seasons, from
Beginning unto infinity, beauty how I believe in
Your essence, thy guiding light into
Tranquility, this peace I have found in thee,
Reflects your radiant energy, as your love has
Grown silently into thy heart indefinitely,
Beauty I must express that in this sacred
Garden lives for you and only you, thy love,
Forever transcending, knowing tomorrow is
No promise, as I love unconditionally, only
You each and every passing day, unto you
Today, and forever unto beauty's garden.

Beauty from Up Above

Beauty from up above, have you fallen from
The sky and landed upon thy heart and soul?
Has your beauty and thy love embraced?
Sublime, directing the unique mysticism of
Your divine elegance my way, has the breath
Of life and love in the air I breathe in,
Signified fire, air, desire, and strength? All in
Time, destiny's elements of beauty from up
Above, created by the creator, reality's
Harmony, spiritually crafted, while mounted
In valiant faith, as I have relied solely upon
Thy soul, a guiding light, leading you my way,
Which was designed from the beauty up above,
Unto the beauty and love within, if I were
Adam, beauty from up above would surely be
My eve, for beauty and love from up above
Have landed upon thy heart and soul
Eternally.

Admire

Oh how I admire thee, as your love has
Opened the closed curtains of thy soul
Spiritually, allowing the grass to grow
Greener, and the sun to shine brighter upon
Thee, it is your beauty that protects your
Strength that nourishes and your love that
Replenishes, when clouds bring tears, that
Water the seeds of our love, and your beauty
Turns rain to sunshine, storms to rainbows, and
Caterpillars to butterflies, oh how I admire
Thee, thy beautiful majestic flower of an
Immortal soul, I hope and dream eternally,
That our love will always continue to
Blossom and grow, oh how I admire thee.

Beauty and Grace

For love lives within beauty, and grace
Within kindness, for she is the light that shines
From within, staring from the windows of her
Soul, creating an unforgettable bond, while in
Search of complete happiness, thus I stare,
Lighting the darkness of thy heart,
Intertwined in spirit, and enraptured by
Delightedness, the essence captivating, but
Life's many rainfalls have caused cold feet, for
Love is genuine, and grace is beauty, this rare
Virtue, of a soulful angel, mysteriously
Represents thee, with profession, discretion,
And sublime reasoning, for love will never be
Forgotten as the footsteps of life's journey
Continue on, unto the parallel road of
Eternity, and the images of this exquisite
Ballad of magical poetry, tells an untold
Story, by the alluring eyes of this precious
Jewel, grace and beauty I thank you, for this
Poem reveals secrets within the eyes of its
Beholder, for the cliche of thy silent
Thoughts of you now, have been laid to rest,
But never spoken by the poet beauty and
Grace.

Almond Eyes

Almond eyes, I can feel your stare, as you
Touch my spirit, and the world from the
Windows of your soul, almond eyes, you are
Life's topaz diamond, allowing our love to
Never grow old, almond eyes, you allow the
Sun to shine, as your clairvoyance holds the
Allure of my heart, tranquil, yet captive and
Mesmerized, composed within the stars, as a
Stream of water flows infinitely from the
Mirrors of a river's pond, your almond eyes
Have entwined with the entity of my soul,
Almond eyes, your celestial arrangement is
Rare as a tropical flower, blowing freely in
The wind, almond eyes, your essence is like no
Other unique creation that was ever meant,
Almond eyes, you are from up above framed a
Statue of beauty's element.

First Place

You are the first in my life, for there could
Be never a second, you are the first thought in
My mind when I rise to see a new day, the first
To say I love you and I miss you eternally, you
Are the first in my thoughts when they run
Through my mind, the first in my soul till the
Never ending of time, you are the first who has
Ever made me feel the way that I do, complete
And secure, reassured and true, you are my
First loyal friend, my first soul mate forever,
The first in my fantasies, as I fanaticize about
You, so first place in my life means I am your
Prize reward love absolute.

Together We Stand

Is it you and I, standing strong for all
Eternity? Is it you and I, standing, searching
For joy and happiness, entwined toward our
Destiny? Is it you and I, set on a course from the
Heavens? Or is it you and I, two souls dancing
in Silence? What is it? Just a casual affair,
Standing under the twinkling stars of a moon
Lit night? Or the vows of life, standing,
Connecting our celestial spirits to the rings
Essence of sunshine? Or is it you and I, as one
Viewing rainbows stretching across the
Infinite blue skies? What is it? The meaning of
You and I? As we dream quietly of one another
Swimming together in the vast oceans of our
Mind, with symmetry connecting our hearts
Soulfully in this life time, here I stand with
Heart and soul in hand, hoping that it's you and
I, so together we both can stand, you and I.

Chapter 5

Infinity

The unlimited extent of time and balance in
Life passes straight through the soul, vast and
Infinite, like an immense vessel in space,
Traveling upon the axis of infinity.

Infinity

An infinite soul,
Traveling amongst time,
Infinity's journey.

The Axis of Infinity

The wind flows swiftly upon life with no
Limits or boundaries, aquatinting itself with
The axis of infinity, this divine truth leads my
Spirit toward a positive attraction, and
Spiritual elevator which sees old age in my
Entity grow wise and true, as each breath of
Air I breathe, the collective union of two,
Become one, and the ever-flowing energy
Unites in this celestial race which has begun
From earth, as I travel up in the shell of life's
Cosmic vessel through infinite cycles, of
Trials and tribulations, adversities, and
Obstacles, searching each expiring day for a
Better tomorrow, my analysis of life I then
Start to ponder, as the final move toward
Relaxation, solitude, and clarity allow my
Soul to reach its destiny upon the axis of
Infinity.

Immortal

In the morning I shall rise with a subtle
Blink, seeing into the eyes of harmony, the
Windows to my soul, infinity, the story of my
Life's magical poetry, an entity written in
Stone, then told, the basic instruction before
Being composed, my reflection, as I stare into
The waterfall, like a mirage in a river's
Stream, mirrors in the shadows of thy
Beginning, the matrix, inevitable, my search
For peace, resting in thy virtual ending, thy
Rose mother of birth, giving me knowledge and
Wisdom to view the world, from my throne, the
Creation I am, an immortal soul.

Wind

A mystic breeze,
Subtle, and ever flowing,
Blowing infinitely.

Limitless and Free

Love flies, limitless and free, amongst the
Calm deep blue skies, soaring with peace and
Inner freedom, as a silhouette of perseverance
And prosperity, limitless and free, purifying
Thy heart with nature's magical poetry,
Adorned by its existence, this manifestation of
Such, energizes thy soul, with true love,
Presenting a stage for relaxing thoughts and
Boundless rhythms, for yesterday, today, and
Tomorrow, true love will fly freely, and live
Peacefully, only in a world where real love
Manifests itself from a caterpillar to a
Butterfly, flying, limitless and free, amongst
Life's infinite blue skies within thee, limitless
And free.

Marriage

The drum beats,
Two pounding hearts,
Tribal dance.

Vows (Part I)

As pebbles lie upon sand unmoved, the
Ambiance of love fills the air, love's aroma of
Life unconditionally connects vows to time, as
Rings of life lines embrace, and are exchanged
In spirit and in heart, for these vows entwine
Us as soul mates, and for you I take these vows,
With understanding and devote faith,
Believing in us, for you I take these vows, from
Beginning, for forever, for never ending, for
You I take these vows, with a promise to
Always love you till death do us part, for you
I take this vow.

Vows (Part II)

Vows which possess our love's truth,
Distinguish what is, and what was always
Meant to be, you and I, these vows are proof,
Understood, and embodied within our
Connecting souls, like two doves that will
Forever fly together in harmony, as one
Unending, making our love's vow above all, the
Rainbow of perseverance, stretching across
The sky, foreseen and glowing in front of many
Eyes and souls, as our vows quietly allow us to
Live out our destiny, under karma's law, divine
For you I take these vows that make you for
Ever mine.

Vows (Part III)

Disguised as a poetic angel of love, for you I
Take these vows, and partake under a starry
Moonlit night, these eternal vows are
Exchanged, lighting the spirit of love and life
While both our souls travel, will you take
These vows infinitely, into the windows of
Your entity, as I take them into mine, living
Our story of written unconditional love,
Unmovable in symmetry, through valleys and
Life's many cycles, all to achieve our true
Goal, everlasting love sealed with vows of
Reality toward destiny, with trust, honor, and
Devotion, shared as two symbolic symbols of
Loyalty's unity, thus for you I take and make
These vows, in mind, heart, body, and soul, till
We lie upon the unmoved sand, share with me,
Into eternal life, these vows.

Love Walks With Me

Love walks with me, as our souls entwine, thy
Heart beats with every whisper of your voice,
The hypnotic affection of harmony, we, us,
Walking hand in hand toward destiny's
Serenity, surrendered to thee, love walks
With me, toward compassion, at life's highest
Peak, the essence of our love's purity, unique,
Embodied spirits peacefully singing, calm
Echoes of thy heart, expresses visions of our
Love, in the twilight of thy dreams, nature's
Infinite unchanging love psalms, sooth thy
Spirit spiritually, the oasis of love forever
Walks with me, like two doves flying, circling
In the skies, immortal beings, soaring amongst
Branches of palm trees, watchful of
Butterflies with spread wings, resting upon
Falls leaves, spring love chimes ring, love
Walks with me, to a realm of ambiance and
Symmetry, our glow an unmovable entity,
Living with chemistry in a sacred garden of
Mystical flowers in the summer blossoming, in
The winter quiet storms may appear, but love's
Circumference will sustain us, step by step,
Under a rainbow of living colors, the sun
Shall shine bright upon us forever, revealing a
Foreseen path, moonlit and illuminating, love
Walks with me, as our love allows our souls
To travel as one into eternity, love walks
With me, forever, beginning to never ending,
Love walks with me.

Chapter 6

Perseverance

The obstacles of human nature convey ways
To the struggles of everyday life. But
Determination and perseverance will lead the
Soul to the pinnacle of the mountaintop.

Perseverance

Over standing life's obstacles,
Possessed with inner strength,
Forever standing strong.

The Mountain Top

At the top of the mountain lies the
Pinnacle of sunshine, with a brief glimpse my
Soul stares, eternally into life's ball of fire,
The all-seeing eye, this reality and life's
Course set to reach the mountain top, will be a
Journey of sheer perseverance, facing
Determination and inner strength, combined
And entwined with the will of one's spirit, deep
Into my vision I explore, as the goal to achieve
My destiny shines brightly amongst the
Infinite blue skies, leading my spirit closer
Each passing day, as my eyes close then awake
To see yet a new day, with faith I continue to
Climb, measuring my dominion, with life's
Allegiance with nature, the mountain top
Becomes closer, my thoughts remain focused,
For I now understand what it takes within, to
Reach the mountain top.

Images

An armored soul,
Freedoms realm,
Serenity's triangle.

Ever Flowing

Within my eyes, is a tale of joy and pain, told
From an ever-flowing soul, in this shell am I,
Covered in silk skin, and birthed from diamond
And coal, my eyes and spirit have seen the
World, viewed by an ancient ever-flowing
Young spirit, I have heard the voices of many
Foolish souls yell, and intelligent minds
Speak, with spiritual conviction, I have
Experienced love and hate, struggle and pain, I
Have cried oceans of tears, and rain, I have
Traveled many miles in thought toward my
Destiny while here, as I continue to expire, day
By day, so with this ever-flowing soul I leave
With you the world this poem, as my spirit, ever
Flowingly lives on, now I turn out the lights
And close my eyes, for now I realize, that my
Spirit is reborn, ever flowing.

Future

The reflection of today,
The replica of tomorrow,
The future.

Significant

Significant other, our love is ever-flowing,
As thy journey in thought, ventures upon the
Waves were the sunsets, connecting destiny
With love, and significant others in heart and
Soul, as hours turn to minutes in our lives,
While minutes present loving you every
Second, the omnipotence significant
Craftsmanship, us, we, love's greatest
Development of significant others entwined in
Life's magical poetry, your essence and spirit is
Significant.

Bells

The bell rings signifying,
An infinite, celestial race,
Joyous moments.

Shooting Star

A flight from above,
The still of night,
Destiny's calling.

Sacred Garden

Earth's soil,
Seeds of life,
Majestic flowers.

Mountains

Staring from a distance unto the statue and
Monument of nature's beauty and pure
Splendor, the mountain, reflects life's replica
Of struggle, strength, and solidarity, all
Consumed up of the soul's destiny and journey
To overcome obstacles, as the spirit climbs to
Reach life's peak upon a rock, versus life's
Adversities, this alone will forever be an
Eternal journey, all to reach the top, and
View the eye of the horizon, peeking then
Staring into the windows of your soul, for
Mountains are unmovable, but determination,
And dedication allows the mountains in life to
Become conquerable.

Chapter 7

Pain

Pain is love, and pain is life, pain will make
You cry, but love will dry your eyes, pain is a
Dark night, under a starry full lit moon, and
Pain is a reflection of a beating heart, in which
Pain has consumed, the pendululum of pain.

Pain

A tear drops,
The rain falls,
Never ending.

The Pendulum of Pain

Pain has struck thy soul like thunder and
Lightning, it has clouded thy heart, as rain
Pours down on thy spirit, flooding thy mind,
Searching patiently for love to appear, the
Only antidote that can cure, what emotions
Feel inside, as pain knocks you off your feet,
And sunshine turns to darkness, happiness stolen
And replaced, then placed upon this pendulum,
While pain stands dignified like a monument,
Perplexing and empty as this may be, lonely is
Thee, knowing within, that pain is like
Shackles placed upon the shadows of thy
Heart following, as love awaits to break free
From the pendulum of pain, that has come over
Thee.

Tears

A story told,
Life's unwanted treasures,
Tears drop.

Empty Hearts

As empty hearts search to be fulfilled, and
Unconscious minds, look for truth in life, but
Still remain blind, journeying upon a path of
Joy and happiness into pain and darkness,
Allures thy empty heart, where echoes of
Traveling souls all conglomerate in search
Of light to lead there way, and then
Eventually resting amongst the wind in ever
Flowing silence, as freedom screams in
Quietness, astonished at this empty heart, that
Has consumed thee, and for just momentarily,
Presenting a presentation of pouring tears,
From the raining heart within, and
Surrounding the seasons within the earth's
Empty bubble, ever turning, thy heart once a
Shooting star, of now and past has landed upon
Soil, life's poetic seed of existence, separated
From love, then sprinkled like ashes, infinitely
Drifting on the surface of the ocean seas, into
The sunset, thy soul cries a smile, then slowly
Lives and dies without love, I am empty.

Darkness

A blind dream,
An unconscious soul,
Eyes open.

The Dynamics of Pain

Love allows the heart to escape the
Dynamics of pain one feels, as thy spirit
Submerges from the depth of pain's captivity,
Once blindfolded was the sight of destiny,
With a broken soul in a realm of anguish,
Distress, and spiritual confusion, yet the
Strength of magical poetry allows thy soul
To escape the pain emotionally, keeping the
Spirit alive, against the forces of an unlit
Tunnel of darkness, and creating feelings of
Numbness, that take away happiness, while
Loneliness is trapped in solitude, the dynamics
Of pain in life passes through and through.

A Silent Cry

In my silent cries, a story is told, a story of
Hurt, pain and sorrow, in those silent cries I am
The story teller, and in my silent cry, is the
Tale of life's unwanted treasures, expressed
From silent places where many years dwell, all
These feelings have been buried deep within my
Heart, all with no road maps, no directions to
Start, with emotion and sadness, confusion and
Fear, I suppose I will begin with the silent cry
Of a tear, a silent cry.

Rain Drops

As the rain drops and pours from the infinite
Dark clouds in the sky, love showers the heart
And soul, pain is no longer caught in life's
Storms, a shelter protects the spirit, like an
Umbrella, the rain drops and pours, but the sun
Shine shall appear again, after the cycle of
Nature is reborn, then a rainbow shall stretch
Across the sky, filled with the many
Experiences of life, all shared all entwined
Amongst life, a new day will come again, and
Rain drops, shall turn to sunshine again.

Tears of a Shadow

The tears that slowly run down my cheek,
Then splash upon my shadow, are also my
Shadows tears, in tears, from many years of
Pain, hurt, struggle, and sorrow, these tears
Are also the tears that fall directly upon my
Shadow, reflecting the hour glass of times
Lived, from yesterdays until tomorrow, my
Tears in my shadow are tears often shaded by
Joy and happiness, which fulfill the moments
In my life, and eliminate the sadness, the
Tears that I have cried many times before,
Tears quietly laid to rest upon a shadow of
Tears that lie upon the floor, the tears of a
Shadow.

The Things I've Lost

The things I've lost can fill the pages of the
Thickest dictionary, and just the thought can
Bring fear to the heart and soul of any man or
Woman spiritually, I can't say that I have lost
Millions, but physically I can say the money I
Have lost has very little importance, I have
Lost countless opportunities, and they all
Seem to be vitally important, but the
Numerous relationships I've lost, were the
Ones I thought would put me to rest,
Relationships with love, and relationships
With future opportunities, but even with such
Tremendous losses, it was not the end, and
When I lost my first love, I didn't think I could
Ever lose again, but eventually I would lose
Years of my life, and at that time it would
Become the most important thing in my life,
And when I think of all the most important
Things I've lost along the way, the one thing I
Have yet to lose is now the most important
Thing in my life, unconditional love for my
Family.

Chapter 8

Struggle

Struggle allows the soul to make great
Efforts in its journey to reach destiny, the
Dynamics in life presents great forces that
The spirit struggles to overcome, thus we must
Never give up, despite the dynamics of life's
Struggles.

Struggle

The trials and tribulations,
Obstacles and adversities,
Better days.

The Dynamics of Struggle

Often clouds may appear, changing the
Course of nature when storms are near,
Sometimes life can be altered, making destiny
Far more unreachable than what was foreseen
To come, yet struggle is our symbol of
Strength, and perseverance allows our spirit
To become an instrument of hope, eluding the
Pouring rain, and the dynamics of sadness and
Pain, thus the sun must shine, and the grey
Clouds must make way for the infinite blue
Sky, as our souls remains entwined amongst
The dynamics of struggle, and the forever
Ticking hourglass of time.

Sunset to Sunrise

As the still of night passes on to the bright
Of day, the resurrection of morning is
Reincarnated, from dusk to dawn, presenting a
New sunrise, and a vibrant energy from the
Eyes of the radiant sun, upon us life shines, yet
A cold cloud of truth remains in the calm blue
Immense sky, while a rainbow mysteriously
Stretches with open arms from its colorful
Beginning, unto its inevitable ending of time,
This sublime given invitation of struggle, from
Sunset to sunrise.

The Sycamore Tree

My soul lies patiently waiting in the grasp
Of darkness, covered in deep frost, but quiet
And still, as my entity, a unique but endangered
Species strives relentlessly to reach its set
Destination, here unfortunately I remain, in
This lost forest, forgotten and trapped in the
Custody of chaos, and solitude beneath the
Erie darkness of the sycamore tree..

Another Cold Morning

As the captured blind eye watches, the
Morning cold spirits yell, roar, and scream,
All in cadence, while footsteps pound, and
Heartbeats repetitively beat, sadly confined,
Hidden secretly in the valleys, mountains and
Deserts of morning, unthawing daily my
Bones, and pipes that squeak and rust loudly,
Then realizing that yet another day has
Passed as the mystical darkness of night does
Not last, thus here I lie covered from head to
Toe, in cloth protecting the flesh from this
Arctic environment, still shivering, for this
Meant-to-be journey has taken its daily coarse,
Unto yet another cold morning.

Alpine's Home

All is quiet, and peaceful in alpine's home, a
Column of sunlight breaks through the clouds,
While nature shines its impression of life's
Elaborate glow upon my soul, the birds fly,
Yet still guard their wildlife with caution
And privacy, wary of intrusion, as my spirit
Shall perform just the same, although blind as
To what may lie ahead, I have now entered
Into alpine's home, where many unprotected
Souls have dwelled, but trustworthy that the
Remote and omnipotent force in life will keep
My soul protected, as this perhaps may be one's
Final dwelling place, all residing amongst
Time, and space, alpine's home, nature's haven,
My soul's wild side's resting place, alpine's
Home.

Pathway

A road of many obstacles,
Choices given in life,
Future outcome.

Our Time

It's our time, to shine as bright as a midnight
Star, it's our time, to live out our destiny that
Was written thus far, it's our time, to grasp the
Horizon and reach for eternity, it's our time,
To reap the rewards of our struggle from
Perseverance, it's our time, to flourish and
Receive the fruits of our success, it's our time,
To attain the reparations from our sacrifice,
It's our time, to live not in pain, but in joy an
Happiness, it's our time, to smile and no longer
Cry, it's our time, to walk in peace by faith upon
The path that was designed and laid, it's our
Time, to love and no longer hate, it's our time,
To unite, our time is now, it's our time.

The Magnitude of Isolation

Isolated and confined in solitude, unable to
Find light in the darkness, yet my soul reaches
Out, as my spirit tries to escape the confines of
Isolation, while the quarters of confinement
Continue to suppress all possible motion and
Mobility, yet my mind runs free, for the
Creation I am, a poetic soul journeying across
The soil of earth and evolving amongst the
Cycle of life between the nucleus of time and
Space, which allows my message to break free
From the magnitude of isolation which has
Confined me.

Never-Ending Freeway

Traveling within the shell of my soul's
Spiritual vessel, I enter upon the on ramp of
Life's never-ending freeway, merging slowly
With caution, I check the rearview in the
Consciousness of my mind, as I stare out of the
Windows to my soul, but blinded by the sun,
Fortunately blessed with the gift of hindsight
And intuition, I avoid collisions and mere
Obstacles of trials and tribulations, all at
High speed, weaving in and out of life's
Happiness and miseries, as time waits for none
Especially living in the fast lane, with the
Divider of truth one simple swerve from fate,
My soul travels at high speed upon life's never-
Ending freeway.

Chapter 9

Destiny

Seasons are lived and seasons will definitely
Change, life will present struggle, and in
Reality you shall find truth in pain, the
Seasons of destiny, four seasons in life we must
All experience and live through.

Destiny

Life's chosen path,
Written in the stars,
Inevitable ending.

The Seasons of Destiny

An immortal soul sits quiet and still, as the
Poetic inclination of reality's intricate
Thoughts race steadily through the mind, for
Survival and strength has led this spirit
Through the many seasons to reach its destiny,
For this lonely soul knows the feeling of cold
Winter rains like tears, what it feels like to
Fall, like the leaves from a palm tree, yet
Still rise back up, to watch the flowers
Blossom and bloom at spring and the sun rest
Upon the sky on a hot summer's sunrise, for the
Many seasons of life, have led this lonely soul
Through the many seasons of life, all to reach
Its final destiny as composed in this poem from
The heart of a lonely soul.

Celestial Race

Moving fast,
The pavement black,
Final ending.

Horizon

Eyes blink,
A distant sunset,
Mountain's peak.

Destination

A young spirit,
An old soul,
The journey of life.

Foreseen

A look into the future,
Visions of destiny,
A captured moment.

Home

A lion's roar,
Gazelle speed,
A fertile land.

Hypnotized

For your love I have been willingly
Hypnotized, placed under your magical poetic
Spell, as I believe no one else can ever make
The sun rise and set in my heart the way you do,
This hypnotism must be a touch of immortal
Love, which has found complete tranquility
And solace within my soul, taking me to love's
Higher realm, and endless harmony, all
Created within eternity, you and I, unmovable
Throughout love's galaxy, for I am hypnotized
By the way you make me feel, and despite space
And time, winter, summer, spring, and fall, your
Love's hypnotism is poetry in motion, and love's
Magical spell, for your love has me forever
Hypnotized.

Y.O.U.

You shape the design of my heart, you fulfill
The desires of my fantasies, you occupy the
Thoughts that run wild in the forest of my
Mind, you allow my hopes and dreams to
Become reality, you take my love and
Together we live unconditionally, you
Connect my soul to yours as we become soul
Mates eternally, you are the reflection of me,
And I of you, as now the world can see, for you
Are you, and that is why my heart and soul
Belongs only to you.

The Petals of My Flower

The petals of my flower, possess many
Different qualities within, from the softness
Of its touch, to the happiness in life it brings,
The petals of my flower, have become a
Reflection of how much my flower means to
Me, as I stare into the beauty in your eyes, or
The diamonds in your wedding ring, for your
Petals possess an infinite glow, shining like
None other that I've ever seen before, my
Flower has stood dignified and tall through
Life's many rainfalls, blowing eternally in
The wind, just as the stars were created, the
Sun and the moon, the petals of my flower will
Forever in my heart, blossom and bloom.

Chapter 10

Prosperity

We often dream of success, and living a happy
And prosperous life, but in these visions, possess a
Soulful message of struggle, life, love and truth,
As our dreams of hope and prosperity carry us
Through until we finally awake, it is those exact
Dreams of happiness that reflect the success of
Our dream's reality.

Prosperity

A soulful vision,
Dreams of success,
Prosperity's destination.

The Dreams of Prosperity

Could life be a dream that I have yet to wake up
From, perhaps reality's final call, maybe our hopes
Are our dream's soul mate and lifetime companion,
Living each day in love and together in life, but
With dreams do come prosperity, if I could only
Awake and grasp my destiny, could our dreams be
Far too actual to reach, yet I fear to never dream,
Because dreams do come true, and dreams do
Become nightmares, waking you up out of a cold
Dream, whatever the conclusion may be, I hope to
Forever daydream, because nothing comes to a
Dreamer but a dream, so wake me when I've
Reached the final destination of my dreams of
Prosperity.

Dreams

Visions within the mind,
Thoughts anticipating reality,
Hopes, dreams.

Picnic

Vintage brass painting,
Basket of love,
Under a tree.

Mirage

Drifting upon a path untraveled, yet in the near
Distance is an ending which has never been
Written, sailing upon the ocean's seas, as the waves
Of life continue to lead the spirit not to land, but
Deeper into the infinite sea, racing a race in search
Of a finish line, starting with determination but
Never finishing in time, living each day in search of
Joy and happiness, only to be consumed by pain and
Sadness, searching for truth and reality, only to
Find lies within our destiny, for the thirst to live
And prosper can often be nothing more than a
Mirage lying in the middle of the dessert.

Reasons

There are many reasons why we do what we do,
What motivates our spirit to rise, and what
Reasons we use to follow through, the reasons
Why each of our life's journeys separate the
Other, the reasons why we endure and love as one
Together, there are reasons why the clouds were
Created in its rare and unique form, reasons why
The sun, moon, and stars, were born, reasons why
Our personalities and characters distinguish us
From one another, the reasons why are, the
Reasons why I continue to search for the answers
To the reasons in my mind, that I hope eventually
To one day discover, the reasons why.

The Authenticity Within

There is an authenticity that lies within, that
Defines the eye, within I, my beginning from my end,
The start from my finish, a pierced spirit from
Repaired and authentic, my love from my hate, my
Joy from my pain, as I once walked in the dark
Through the storms and the rain, my light in the
Night, my flame, from my spark, there is an
Authenticity that lye's within, which defines my
Entity at heart, that is created authentic from
Deep within, for my soul is authentic and
Defined in my spirit.

First Degree

Without pain, I wouldn't have motivation,
Without hurt, I wouldn't know serenity, without
The creator, my body wouldn't be in its unique
Form, without long suffering, I wouldn't be
Thankful for peace, without danger, I wouldn't
Know the essence of safety, without struggle, I
Would have no reason to push forward in life,
Without pride, I wouldn't have the strength to
Stand up nor rise, instead I would flee run and hide,
Without failure, my heart wouldn't have the
Ambition to succeed, without faith, my spirit would
Be weak, without inspiration, I would
Underachieve, without the almighty omnipotent
One, we wouldn't know love in the first
Degree.

Before It's Too Late

Before it's to late, I must let you know that I
Love you, before I once was blind and could not
Truly see the value of our love eternally, nor the
Unconditional truth of your love in which you
Have possessed my heart with, now the sun shine
Within the essence of your beauty glows intensely,
From the windows of your soul, unto the windows
Of mine, together forever these virtues are pure
And beautiful, thus I cherish the fantasies we share
As they have now become a reality and true, so
Before now I never understood you and I forever
And the true meaning of love's unconditional
Truth, but now I do, before it becomes too late,
I must let you know that I love you.

Commitment

With this commitment I shall make a vow of you
And I forever, to possess your heart I would take
Each and every ounce of my love and pour it
Slowly upon your unconditional heart and soul, and
With this commitment that means forever,
Although life is not perfect this commitment
Shall always remain pure, for I shall love with all
That I can and will ever possibly be, as this is my
Justification of my love's clarity, and my honor of
Your love eternally, rather for richer or poorer,
Through sickness and health, rain or shine, joy and
Pain, this commitment to you shall last forever as
I plan to walk with you hand and hand up to the
Aisle in the clouds and forever resting with the sun,
Moon, and stars this is my commitment to you.

Chapter 11

Romance

Life's epic tale of romance, can send quivering
Vibrations to any of love's captivated hearts and
Souls, as mysterious as this may be, the vibrations
Of romance is as extraordinary as your life's epic
Tale of love and the vibrations of romance in
Symmetry.

Romance

An enchanting proposal,
Of suave seduction,
Captivated souls.

The Vibrations of Romance

The vibrations of romance forms love's divine
Unity, then formulates a light allowing energy to
Flow through the souls of two spirits enraptured
In the feeling of ecstasy and captivity, for these
Vibrations are felt deep within the heart the
Moment romance is compelled and vibrations are
No longer afar, growing deeper and becoming
Boundless as the essence fills the room and blooms
Like a precious flower on a spring day awakening
At the strike of noon, therefore close your eyes
And you shall feel the vibrations of romance,
Growing deeper and deeper inside your heart and
Soul, vibrating until romance has you completely
Consumed.

Fireplace

The fireplace creates crisp thoughts,
As lit candles burn quietly,
Igniting romance.

When Passion Pursues Immunity

When passion pursues immunity, the journey of
Love connects souls eternally, love becomes a
Frontline soldier, and passion becomes an
Instrument of destiny, and then, and only then, will
Passion breathe freely, as the leaves fall quietly
From the trees, while the earth is vehemently
Turning and nature's symmetry, synchronizes with
The essence of passion's symphony, possessed within
Ecstasy, but commanding of this chase for
Immunity, only to elude pain and emptiness briefly,
Life's pursuit of love, passion's pursuit for
Immunity.

Where I Wanna Be

With you is where I wanna be, as time leads us on
Into the sunrise and we hold on to the
Unconditional highs and lows of life's sunset, with
You is where I wanna be, living in the serenity of
Your heart, and feeling the tranquility of your
Presence, while we sail as one into the abyss of
Never ending love, never taking for granted each
And every moment spent in spirit together, against
The allure of life itself, but climbing mountains
Under the vows of our umbrella, eluding the
Pouring rain, as each day passes us by, with you is
Where I wanna be, looking deep into your soul's
Eye, where love reflects no darkness, only light
Shining into the spectrum of my soul, faithful and
True, with the love I have forever dreamed of,
Where I wanna be is only with you.

Chemistry

Love's divine connection,
Entwining the spirit,
As one.

A Gift

The intense vibes of your affection I hold
Tightly, like a gift from the heart, the diary of
Our love I embrace, happily ever after, the
Imagination of your essence in my thoughts run
Wild, as the transformation of your affection,
Personifies a glow within my soul, the blend of
Your clairvoyance of beauty I adore, and the
Journal of your innovative strength, is absorbed
By the atmosphere, as the dedication of your love
Is a gift from up above, for you are that special
Gift, in the essence of love.

Taken

Captivated by romance,
Captured by ecstasy,
Spiritually taken.

Vibrations

Beating of the heart,
Vibrations in the soul,
Igniting romance.

Recapture and Recreate

If I could recapture your love, I would
Sacrifice the world, smash a universe, and recreate
Our eternity, if I could recapture and recreate
The times we've shared, I would cherish
Every wonderful moment we've ever spent, and
Secure the abundance of our love through
Prosperity and perseverance, if I could recapture
And recreate, then duplicate, but never fade away,
The fact that the quality of our beings was
Created and meant to be, then who could question
The love that we've recaptured and together
Recreated forever and everlasting.

Chapter 12

Eternity

Eternal life is achieved when one's deeds, are
Remembered and last forever throughout many
Life times, and also when one has planted seeds in
The everlasting garden of eternity and life.

Eternity

A never-ending course,
Traveled with no beginning,
Everlasting existence.

The Seeds of Eternity

You are my seeds of eternity, therefore my spirit
Shall live for all eternity, and my soul shall
Continue to travel the earth's soil on its never-
Ending life's journey, you are my seeds for an
Eternity, therefore I shall keep achieving all my
Hopes and dreams, like an eagle set free, I will
Continue to soar amongst the clear blue skies in
Search of my eternity, at the end of my struggles,
You are my seeds to eternity, thus each breath you
Breathe, I breathe and as you search for eternal
Life in the next generation of you and I, for you are
My seeds of eternity and as long as our souls
Continue to manifest in our seeds, our spirit and
Deeds of this infinite virtue will live for all
Eternity.

Majestic Flower

My majestic flower, you are and will always be
My one and only, majestic flower, growing in the
Most beautiful image of I, my first-born leader to
Blossom, bloom, and rise, through all four seasons,
From a seed planted in the garden of eternal life,
You have delivered my spirit happiness, and
Brought my heart and soul so much joy, and
Overwhelming delight, the moment I first laid my
Eyes upon you I realized, the beauty you possess
Within, in the form and creation of the creation I
Am, my majestic flower, never stop blowing in the
Wind, as you are the keeper and soul reflection of
The creation I am within, as you are in divine
Possession of my heart forever, rather I, in spirit,
Or I, in thought, I will forever and a day hold on to
Your hand in hand and occupy your majestic heart,
Till you reach your destiny in eternity, for your
Energy illuminates the world and glows as bright
As the midnight star shining over the infinite
Ocean's sea, thus when I stare into the windows of
Your soul's majestic eyes, I will forever see myself
In the image of you and I, I shall love you forever
Till the never-ending end, my majestic flower
Eternally blowing in the wind.

Unbreakable

Your spirit and soul is unbreakable, and your
Heart has been filled with eternal love and
Prosperity unconditional, as your time to become
The next spiritual instrument and leader of hope
Will surely come, you are and will always be my
Ambition of eternal existence sent here to spread
Love, joy, and happiness upon this cold world, you
Are a warrior in your prime, my seed planted in the
Garden of eternal life, destine to grow and
Prosper as you must awake each day and rise, rise
With courage and strength and carry on our
Pillar of endurance and unbreakable
Perseverance, for you are the creation I am, and
Through you I will always be, unbreakable and
Forever everflowing.

Forever

An endless journey,
Eternal in time,
Forever young.

A Young Heart

A young heart beats quietly to the melody of
Nature's song, unmoved amongst all that is
Moveable, quiet and still, yet full of ambition, the
Fire burns within, igniting an inner flame that is
Ever flowing to the symmetry of life, this young
Heart co-exists with love and all harmony,
Expressed through magical poetry, with an old
Soul lying in the distance, pounding but awakened
To the poetic subject of a young beating heart
That will live for all eternity, the beating of a
Young heart.

Good Bye

Good bye doesn't always mean forever, good bye
Doesn't always mean that we want ever again be
Together, so with this good bye, I hope that we will
See one another again, in the life after, good bye
And may our life, love and joy bring us peace
Forever, good bye.

Jewels

You are my diamond, you are solid as gold, you
Are like jewels of eternal life, I shall live forever
And never grow old, for I have handed down to you
In spirit and soul, the jewels of eternal life, my
Knowledge and wisdom in the jewels of this poem,
I have revealed the truth to you in there lies, all in
The words I have composed, just close your eyes,
Then listen to my voice and read my poetry as it
Shall unfold, as I quietly speak the words that
Explain, these jewels, the truth about nature,
Love, and life, struggle and pain, how to survive
Past, present, and future experiences, exactly
What all of this means, are the jewels of many life
Lines that are now passed down to you from me.

Night Star

Darkness, can never be darkness, as long as you
Shine bright as a night star, for you will one day
Stand alone my night star, and will never fall
From the sky, continue to glow amongst the
Infinite consolations, and moon in which with you
Complete the sky, for you light up the galaxy,
Shine my eternal night star struggling with life
And love all in harmony, share your message with
The universe all by the twinkle in your eye, then
Allow the sun to seize the morning's sunrise, thus
Never allow darkness to overcome night my night
Star, forever shine your light wherever you are,
Shine bright my night star, shine bright.

Bouquet of Roses

My rose, this poetic bouquet is composed for you,
As your love will forever remain a pillar of fire
And perseverance in my heart and soul, burning
Uncontrollably for many years to come, for your
Strength has been passed down to me, and the
Virtues of your inner being I shall carry with me
Forever and all eternity, you have shown me
Unconditional love and strength, now those
Jewels live within my entity, as this is where life
Started for me, my thoughts of you will continue
To blossom and bloom each and every time I think
Of you, my rose, my heart and soul, this bouquet of
Roses is for you as I have composed my love for you
In the form of a poem, my rose.

Chapter 13

Loneliness

Loneliness can shatter the windows of one's
Soul, chills can create shivers within the heart,
Melting slowly away at ones hopes and dreams of
Reality, all these experiences within solitude, but
The power of love will forever warm the spirit
And soul from the chills of loneliness.

Loneliness

Enclosed in confinement,
Solitude within seclusion,
Standing alone.

The Chills of Loneliness

Lost in a dark room, my spirit slowly drifts
Into forgotten pain, as the chills of
Loneliness indefinitely conquer
Strategically with victory my soul, I search
For a way out, yet my body shivers as the
Conductor of this lonely heart whispers
Thoughts of complete sadness which remain
Framed in the memory of my mind, thus I shiver,
While tears run down my cheek like
Waterfalls, splashing darkness upon the walls
And floors of this lonely encased
Environment, thus I shiver, searching for the
True antidote and real meaning of comfort
And peace, yet still shivering, as one day the
Chills of loneliness will be the gateway into
Eternal happiness, fulfilling my soul with
Warmth and energy eternally, yet still the
Chills of loneliness continue to follow
Me.

Chills

Shivers within the heart,
Restless feelings from thoughts,
Unbalanced emotions.

Without You

Without you, love would have no meaning,
Without you, my heart would beat flat line
With no feeling, without you, the sun would
Never rise within me, without you, darkness
Would forever overcome thee, without you,
Eternal life could never exist, or I be free, and
The seeds of our eternity would be non-
Existent you see, without you, joy would
Forever be pain, without you, my life would be
Lived in vain, without you, my day would
Always be night, my life would be cloudy, and
The sun would never shine, without you, times
Would forever be hard, happiness would be
Struggle, and my life could never be complete
Or enjoyed, so I am blessed to never be without
You, my soul mate I can't live a day of my life
Without you.

Abandoned

Cold chills at night,
Shivers in the heart,
Abandoned soul.

With You

With you, I live each and every day captured
In the rapture and captivity of your
Unconditional love, while together we view
Life's portrait through the windows of our
Connected souls, with you, loneliness is only a
Mere fragment of my imagination, because
With you, I am complete and whole and can
Never be severed by a broken heart, with you, I
Have seen the visions that true beauty has to
Offer, and divine love all in you, allowing me
Strength to overcome, with you, the sun will
Forever shine upon my spirit, for my search for
A soul mate has finally ended, with you.

The Entity of the Heart

My heart beats, and often skips a beat with
The impulse of struggle, as it searches for
Fulfillment at the divine request of love, for
This is not the work of the mind, but the
Creative design within the entity of the heart,
Finding its way through life's complex and
Perplex maze, beating intensely, yet pounding
In complete silence, in its life course to elude
Captivity, and misery, then pumping blood
Through vessels and life lines in the veins, for
The entity of the heart continues to beat for
All eternity.

The Kiss

An evening walk in the riches of an endless
Night, as the wind blows quietly in the breeze,
Slowly rekindling our fire, holding hands
With each step under the dark, as the light of
Day has abandoned the sunrise and now made an
Epic presentation for our mood under the
Twinkling stars and moon, love is viewed
Intensely from the windows of our soul, as it
Races from our veins to the forefront of our
Thoughts, with anticipation feelings grow
Stronger, and emotions more intense, all to
Reach the final moment of that one special
Kiss.

Echoes

Voices reaching out from within,
Messages left in the consciousness,
Silent echoes.

Broken

Shattered into pieces like a broken glass
Crashing against a concrete floor is my
Broken heart, as I try to swallow life I still
Choke at the feeling of pain and hurt, yet I
Take a deep breath, despite the puddles of my
Tears that slowly drip from my cheek upon my
Shadow lying on the soil of earth, drowning
My soul, as this broken heart has snapped my
Spirit in half, not by the waves drifting into
The infinite sea, but by a broken heart that is
Unable to be mended internally, broken.

Chapter 14

Balance

In life the scales of balance are weighed upon
The spirits determination to persevere and
Prosper against struggle, thus I have come to
Realize that once balance is obtained and the
Scales in our lives are equally balanced, then
Life becomes a joyous experience and love
Becomes the greatest force of all.

Balance

The scales of measures,
Dimensions of life,
Balance, harmony.

The Scales of Balance

When day turns to night and night resorts
Back to day, my soul ponders upon the scales
That balances my life's entity, will
Unconditional love outweigh the world's
Uncontrollable hate, will joy in the morning
Be overcome by night with struggle and pain,
Will the enlightenment of the truth, be
Conquered by secrets and lies, will my trust
Become diluted by deception and demise, will
Reality, eventually lead my spirit to its
Destiny, will sacrifice deliver me to
Prosperity, or will my strengths become my
Weakness, and obstacles be overcome by
Perseverance, will I rise to just fall all over
Again, will my inner endurance find victory in
Reassurance and harmony, or will this cold
World break me and never allow me to be free,
Will my essence continue to glow, or will
Karma destroy me and turn my whole world
Dark for sure, will life respond to my call for
Balance in this reality that is harsh, or will it
Ignore me, as I continue to struggle for the
Scales that bring me balance and eternity, in
The end what will it be, when all is placed
Upon the scales that balance my entity.

Today

Today I rose wondering,
What exactly today may hold,
As I live for, another today.

Unmovable

When rain drops come crashing down like
Tears running wild, we have remained
Unmovable, when grey clouds fill the empty
Skies and truth versus lies occupy the mind, we
Have remained unmovable, when floods of
Negative thoughts overflow like a river's
Stream, and clouds fog our vision, we have
Remained unmovable, when nightmares become
Dreams of reality, we have remained
Unmovable, when obstacles start to overcome
The spirit, and crush our emotions and feelings
Within, we have remained unmovable, when
Love makes our heart skip a beat, and flat line
Lies in the near distance lurking, we have
Remained unmovable, and we shall remain
Unmovable, when loneliness, stress and
Anxiety try to conquer and subdue our
Consciousness, we will remain unmovable, for
Our unconditional loyalty and love for one
Another shall forever remain till death do us
Part unbreakable and unmovable.

Melody

The voices that sing from within,
The melodies that play from the heart,
Rhythmic soul.

Kinetic Souls Entwine

Kinetic souls entwine, as the voices of force
And energy connect, and combine love's virtue
Sublime, this fruitful gift of magical poetry
Allows kinetic souls to dream, as this meant-
To-be moment in life attracts love's magnetic
Energy, while listening to the hummingbirds
Sing, and doves take flight kinetic souls compel
With willing captivity then entwine.

Amazing

You are amazing, for your style and grace
Exemplify pure clairvoyance and strength,
The way you have captured my heart and soul
Through the dedication and perseverance of
Your unconditional love and loyalty, makes
Your entity the symbol and definition of
Amazing, the fabric of your spirit is the peace
That dwells deep within my tranquil thoughts,
The warmth of your loving embrace shelters
Me from the cold and rain, for you are so
Amazing that no one could ever take your
Place, why because your spirit, is amazing.

The Way

The way, you smile brings joy to my heart,
Your stare brings fantasies to my thoughts,
The way, you love fills my soul unconditional,
And the way, you touch completes me deep in
My spirit eternal, for the way, you have shown
Me you, allows my feelings to be free and my
Emotions to capture reality, as the way, we
Were created could only have been for one
Another and that is the reason why I believe
And have faith in you, the way, I do, forever.

Umbrella

Protected from life's hurt and pain,
Guarded from nature's storms and rain,
Beneath life's umbrella.

Rock

A pebble upon sand,
Strength to endure,
Concrete soul.

Chapter 15

Clarity

In every moment of truth, there is an
Opportunity for the spirit, and soul to find
Clarity, to live and breathe freely, sojourning
On this place of momentary peace at the peak of
The tabernacle of clarity.

Clarity

A moment of truth,
Spoken from the soul,
Free spirit.

The Tabernacle of Clarity

Clarity lies within the soul, as the truth
Of life rests in the poetic verse of this poem,
For the goal to reach the tabernacle of
Clarity, flags a truth that only one can reach
In life by clearing the mind and cleansing the
Spirit, take that step upon the mountain top
And the soul will grasp the tabernacle of
Clarity and then you will become free within
Your entity, the tabernacle of clarity, truth
That lies within the depths of your soul in
Clarity.

Last Request

As the incense burns, and fills the aroma
Of this mystic eclipse of life, an old soul
Patiently waits to be laid to rest upon an
Earthly grave, asking for only one
Request, a final closure to what was
Unsaid and left far behind, forgiveness, no
To the last request, yet you still call for
My spirit, but I shall only respond to the
Thoughts that you once left behind,
Absence, these abandoned memories of
Who you are, thus today I shed not a tear
For you thus far, no remembrance, no
Compassion, nor sudden images, only one
Sad life time experience, as I have always
Wondered, why my role model and
Presence in your life was missing,
Unfortunately your request for this final
Call will never be granted, and will
Forever be denied, for your last request is
To rest in peace now, as you slowly fall
Out of life, and leave me far behind, rest in
Peace.

Cleveland Kincade

Truth

Eyes wide open,
Light shining bright,
Spirit knowing truth.

Windows of the Soul

Through the windows of the soul, my
Spirit has seen life as my flesh has lived
Life, not to its fullest, but to the best of
Life that each breath has handed to me,
Through the windows of my soul is an
Entity that has traveled through many
Life times, to deliver many messages, yet in
The windows of the soul, is a reflection of
Who I am, a poetic soul, staring at you
From the windows of the soul.

Karma

Live a humble and prosperous life,
Know that doing wrong is not right,
Karma is life.

How I Feel for You

How I feel for you, can never truly be
Explained only expressed through poetry,
And with my every emotion from the heart
Igniting the flames of love which burn
Like a candle of fire in my soul, for
Nothing compares to you, and no other can
Capture nor captivate the effect of your
Presence, how I feel for you, is an
Unconditional feeling of love that I
Dream each and every day will never go
Away, and last for all eternity, and this is
How I feel for you.

Moments

Times that are shared,
Opportunities that are lost,
Life's moments.

Flow

Let it flow, like the gentle breeze that
Flows in the wind, let it flow as smooth as
The thoughts that allow the ink to drip
Slowly from a pen, let it flow, like the
Rhythmic sound of a seductive melody
Which captivates one's ear, let it flow,
Like the words of unconditional love
Delivered straight from the heart and
Soul, allowing life to let you pass
Through all of the good and conquer the
Majority of the bad, fluently traveling
Down the streams of all to bear, with a
Poetic flow and sense of an immortal soul
That journeys amongst the air, let it
Flow.

One Day

One day I will reach for the sun and
Shine bright as the summer's day, one day I
Shall achieve all my hopes and dreams as
It has always been my destiny, one day
Freedom will allow me to actually
Become free, for one day I will live
Through my seeds and deeds in life for all
Eternity, one day all of these thoughts,
Visions, and aspirations in my mind will
Eventually become reality, one day all of
These desires will come true and no
Longer be a fantasy, one day.

Chapter 16

Change

Change allows trust that the spirit and
Soul within will now lead, for the rest of
One's life unto eternity, as it no longer
Follows in the physical form, this
Transition all from within is determined
By one entity alone, you, then the
Transition all from the soul, allows one
To finally be at peace, a process for all
Who seek change for a better tomorrow
And future prosperity.

Change

The understanding of today,
The realization of tomorrow,
The final call.

The Transition of Change

Change has become the greatest
Accomplishment an entity traveling upon
The soil of earth can ever achieve,
Through change it has allowed my soul to
See destiny and reality more clearly,
Change has allowed my spirit to deliver
This poetic message to the world with my
Magical poetry, change has allowed me
To build family unity, and spread love to
Society, change has allowed my flesh to
Overcome many obstacles and forms of
Adversities, for this transition is not one
That is attained overnight, but one that is
Formulated throughout my life, so don't
Be afraid to walk with your shadow as one
Through the transition of change, it just
Might save your life, and set your spirit
Free.

Transition

Changing life's course,
A new direction,
Spiritual growth.

Tomorrow

Tomorrow is never promised,
Thus, today I live in the moment,
As I live for a better tomorrow.

Listen

As I listen to my thoughts, they quietly
Speak of ambition, determination, and
Prosperity, as I feel the beating of my
Heart, it beats for kindness, joy, love, and
Happiness, as I hear the whispers in my mind,
They speak secretly, whispering strength
Into my soul, as I listen to my spirit speak
This unique but understood language, it
Speaks of survival, destiny, infinity, and
Tranquility, as I search through the
Thoughts in every corner of my mind, I
Hear words of knowledge, wisdom, and
Insight, as I hear my spirit speak to my
Inner consciousness, I understand the
Truth, as I touch bases with the essence of
My entity I feel it expressing the desire to
Change with clarity, with all these
Conversations running through my mind,
All I have to do now, is just listen.

Lost Innocence

Aware of the many truths,
No longer a blind youth,
Conscious mind.

Visions

Many visions have set within the depth of
My spiritual mind, as my soul has looked
Vividly upon the sky, even after I turn off
The lights, these visions still seem to be
My guiding light in the darkness, as I
Search for the answers to these visions
Which I possess, which one day I hope will
Become a reality laid to rest, I believe
That they are formulated by keen
Foresight and not just a foggy vision
Which dwells deep in my spiritual mind,
These visions have sent my spirit on many
Never-ending journeys in life, and now
These visions are clear as day and night,
Thus I close my eyes and visualize, all in
My quest to find the truth, amongst the
Visions I possess in my spiritual mind.

Street Light

A light in the darkness,
Souls lurking amongst night,
Blinded visions.

The Yard

In my yard, green grass grows but soon
Turns weatherbeaten and old, in my yard,
No flowers blossom nor bloom at spring,
As the path I have walked on, is filled with
Asphalt and concrete, while nature's
Predators remain in solitude and prey
Upon the weak, in my yard, the hawk
Watches the birds play and socialize with
A keen eye, as thirst lingers upon his
Tongue and drips from his beak, ants build
Ant holes to navigate their daily demise
For their queen, in my yard, echoes yell
From the soil above earth, and below where
Many unforgotten souls lie, due to many
Years sacrificed, is this perhaps the gift
And the curse, as I am welcomed to the
Yard amongst loneliness, stress, and
Chaos, as these emotions remains the scent
Of drama and despair, the yard I have woken
Up every morning to, has now changed me
Within, and made my dreams come true all
With a breath of morning fresh air.

Ready

I'm ready, to be everything that I was
Created and designed to be, I'm ready, to
Live out my hopes and dreams, as life rides
My soul and entity into the sunset of all
Eternity, I am now ready, to never feel
Hurt nor pain, only pure love, joy, and
Happiness that is unconditionally secure, I
Am ready, to move mountains, travel
Through valleys, and sail across the
Waves of many ocean's seas, to achieve all
My desired blessings that have been
Written in the skies above for me, I am
Ready, to love all that needs to be loved,
As I live each and every day in love with
The stars, sun, and moon in harmony, I am
Now ready, to live free and forever, as I
Share with the world my message
Composed within my magical poetry, I am
Now ready.

Chapter 17

Existence

The ambition of existence is passed on
From generation, to generation, and then
The desire to succeed and prosper allows
This determination to exist, which is
Exemplified within the essence of the
Heart and soul of the entity in which we
Are, this is our will to survive, and our
Ambition to exist forever.

Existence

The time taker,
Hopes, and dreams,
Destination's purpose.

The Ambition of Existence

To exist, and prosper with a fearless
Ambition, is my soul's destiny, as my spirit
Searches each and every day for a better
Tomorrow, and I strive to rise at sunrise
And then rest in peace at the end of my
Life's sunset, many struggles and
Adversities I have met with, as time slowly
Expires and the clock continues to keep
Ticking, the hour glass of time runs on
Infinite and eternally, thus the ambition
Of my existence is to spread love, and my
Magical poetry, with joy and happiness
Across the world till my time has ended
And the ambition of my existence is no
Longer left here on earth, but to you
Whom this poem may concern I leave
These jewels with you as a token of my
Existence and love, as I was sent to you,
From up above.

Rose Garden

Rose, my one single stem rose, who rose
From strength and stands dignified
Amongst life, and all other flowers in the
Rose garden of my heart, your love has
Blossomed life into my soul, and your
Beauty has bloomed sunshine into my
Spirit, for you have given me life, so every
Day at sunrise I give thanks for the rose
Whose beauty has flourished from the soil
Of life and the eternity of the rose
Garden of my heart, so forever will I
Cherish you, for you are my rose, my one
Single stem rose, growing each day in the
Rose garden of my soul.

Ambition

A fire burning within,
An aspiring desire,
Serenity's peak.

The Unification of Brotherhood

Brothers, the fire that burns within me,
Burns intensely within you, brothers, the
Same blood that runs through my veins,
Runs through you, I too have been wounded
By the trials and tribulations of life, yet
Still I remain by your side, brothers, the
Ambition that continues to drive me, must
Continue to inspire, motivate, and drive
You, you see brothers, your hopes and
Dreams, are my reality's in search of our
Destiny, brothers, I will never betray you,
As I know that the world has so many
Times lied to me and you, for you are my
Brothers, in flesh, struggle, and soul,
Keepers of one another, as our strength
Shall walk together and then summon our
Shadows, for tills is the unification of
Brotherhood, brothers united, and loyal
Standing forever strong through and
Through.

People

People, moving all in one life's turn
Infinitely, like the breeze of an ocean's
Wind, blowing in its quietest form,
Passionately driving with caution, their
Vehicles within them, unaware of
Warning signs, dark tunnels following
Life, all in search of light, a truth, the
Answer to life's many questions, all while
Taking long walks in life together, and
Often brief runs, toward separate roads,
Others bicycle through the matrix of time,
Headed for cliffs and mountains, or even a
Walk on the pier where the sunsets sublime,
People, chasing life amongst karma, all
For what their souls believe in, a
Spiritual journey already entwined in the
People's spirit, just look at the gift within,
People.

People Everywhere

There are people everywhere and
Nowhere, all living within the four
Seasons of life, from beginning to never
Ending, climbing mountains, reaching for
Life's peaks, rather in love, or in peace,
These poetic souls of philanthropy, all
Connect in spirit holding hands and,
Standing in humanity as one, towering
Abroad and vast, there are people
Everywhere and nowhere, strangers,
Loved ones, here one minute, gone the
Next, there are people struggling, and on
The inside crying, but still believing, in
Hope and faith their life's journey
Toward prosperity, there are people on
The inside smiling, joyous and happy, there
Are people jogging marathons in their
Lives, some overcoming the allure of life,
Others becoming addicted to life, there is
So much that goes on with the people,
Everywhere, here and there, everywhere,
And nowhere, what am I to say, as the
World turns there are people existing, and
Evolving everywhere.

I Am People

I am people, starving for love, peace and
Attention, searching and reaching for the
Sky, my replenishment, the start from the
Earth to up above will be my finish, all in
Good spirit, for I am people, living till I
Eventually perish, and so on, and so on,
Each day as a tourist of this world, I am
People, trapped in the solitude of my
Thoughts, this modern-day college of
Business, and nature's law, fighting against
The divide-and-conquer theory, a thesis of
Stagnation, and hidden secrets, emotions
And feelings that change like the wind, I
Am people, communicating with poetic
Verse, my voice and messages written in
Spoken word, all which keeps the spirit
Alive, from the eyes of peoples' eye, I am
People, and I am a part of you people,
Traveling in life's matrix of infinite time,
For I am people.

The Unseen

The unseen, accompanied with a tug of
Life and embrace, allows control from
The sky's surface to paint a vintage
Portrait of the blue skies before the
Clouds set and the mist fills the air, then
Embraces the moments shared with a
Loved one, versus the memories of
Moments missed, unto the day our souls
Perish, this celestial ride from the
Heavens, unto the meant-to-be moment we
Meet, all up until death, do, us, part, then
Back up above once again, to fall back
Down like a star, remembering with déjà vu
The vows and promises that were
Made back on earth, as the ocean's waters
Replenish, then give birth to the unseen
Cycle of life and time travel over and
Unseen, over again.

Silent Thoughts

A story is always and forever told, of
Silent thoughts laid to rest from the
Still of a silent thought's soul, as a silent
Thought presents strength to endure,
Where all silent thoughts seem to embrace
Emotions and feelings of joy and pain,
Paper allows a silent thought sunshine
And rain, when silent thoughts touch,
Secrets are composed, within the silence
Of its beholder, this inspirited whisper of
A poetic poem all in silence, as tears
Trickle upon paper, embracing sadness and
Puddles turn into tear drops of happiness,
When silent thoughts touch paper, life
Can be expressed through victory and love
Of words can be left without a trace,
Professed in devote faith, when silent
Thoughts embrace, life responds, hope is
Welcomed and dreams reach for reality,
Survival reveals truth by fact, as a new
Freedom is born, a story is always and
Forever told when silent thoughts
Embrace upon paper and the words unfold,
All from a silent thought, from the still
Of a silent thought's soul.

Chapter 18

Life

Life is what you make and create of it,
And life's perception is summed up and
Perceived by the one who is living life
And others who view you existing in life,
So live your life to the fullest, because
You are who you are, and you only get one
Opportunity to be that person in the
Realm of your life's perception.

Life

The first breath taken,
Existing within time,
The last breath given.

Life's Perception

Life's perception can be perceived and
Viewed from many different angles, but
Life's perception can only be explained
From the individual living in life's point of
View, rather life has presented an endless
Journey in life, as struggle is understood
Between wrong and right, or an endless
Motion from an infinite soul, traveling
Between principalities that are
Completely spiritual, as life's perception
Is perceived through the many of eyes
That dwell within the existence of life,
All seen from the windows of the soul
Aware of darkness versus the light, life is
What you make it, and your story is told
From your perception of you living life, as
Your life unravels with time and
Indefinitely unfolds.

Life Changes

As life changes, hopes and dreams strive
To reach for reality, then change adjoins
Eternity, while life slowly captures
Prosperity, all in one life's change, this
Simple but diverse travel amongst the
Atmosphere of the infinite deep blue sky,
Presents infinity in this realm of life's
Chemistry, all in one life's change, a path
Awakened from darkness by truth, but
Ventured through deception, as I the
Vessel, and life the conductor, provides
The essential substance of a soulful
Challenge overcome by all obstacles and
Adversities, in one life's change.

Light

Soaring through time,
Awakened by truth,
Guiding light.

This Place

There is a place, where life has placed the
Message of destiny and reality within the
Soul's vessel, in this place lies a vehicle,
That revolves amongst the crashing
Waves of many ocean seas, and many souls
In life travel with stories that are yet
Told, there is a place where love savors
The sweetness of beauty, where footprints
Are never washed away by the many waves
That crash upon the white sand, there
Lives a place, were shooting stars live on
Forever and tomorrow, this place lives
Alive, in memory and in spirit, where love
Sprinkles life from a fountain, this statue
Represents magical poetry, there lives a
Place within this place, within you and
I.

The Sea

The aquarium of eternal life,
An infinite river's stream,
Nature's portrait.

The Past

As thy soul strives to escape, the past
Seems to live within the entity of the
Present, while on thy quest for eternal
Life, I hope and dream each and every
Passing day for a brighter future, and to
Escape the past, as I drift into the clouds,
Stretching my inner most intricate
Thoughts peacefully across the infinite
Blue skies, yet my past watches, and
Steadily haunts my soul, always creeping,
Rather far or near, night or day, yet I
Search for understanding, while trapped
As a slave and refugee of the past.

Life's Expedition

As life's expedition navigates thy soul
With a guiding light of resilience, a glow
To see life shine within, blinds the
Darkness and the strength to overcome
Obstacles, presents a unique mentality
Believing spiritually, that the direction
Of life's expedition will eventually
Present a portrait of beauty and love, at
The end of this lifetime crusade, over
Mountains, valleys, and ocean seas, the
True sight of pure splendor and vintage
Creativity, seen clearly by the soul's
Essence upon life's expedition, carrying
Magical poetry as its never-ending
Message.

Life's Abyss

As thy spirit drifts solemnly amongst the
Tides of life's abyss, sailing indefinitely in
Search of an infinite passageway unto
Your heart and soul, this overwhelming
Feeling of life's entwined entities, reveal
The tenderness and clairvoyance of love's
Essence and the pitfalls of life's
Temptations, the abyss of harmony and
Vanity, despite time and space, together as
One we breathe, while our love remains
Floating yet existing soulfully, but our
Emotions are weightless upon a pendulum
That comes and goes constantly, and the
Wind blows quietly in peace, as it realizes
The fact of life's abyss caged in penance,
Sorrow has enjoyed the pitfalls of life's
Endless company, now thy soul must sail
On into life's abyss, eternally.

Life's Cycle

The wind blows a tumbleweed across the
Desert floor, the sun shines during the
Day, as the stars sparkle evermore, the
Moon glows under the starry constellation
Of night, flowers bloom in spring, as the
Summer presents the cycle of life, the
Birds fly during the day, and a rainbow
Stretches across the sky, over the
Mountaintop is where I view the horizon,
The reflection of you and I, a waterfall
Splashes against the rocks, as the tides
Crash against the sand, the sky opens up
From light to darkness, and the truth is
Reincarnated by man, these are life's
Cycles, nature's common laws, magical
Poetry in the making, life's cycles in
Spiritual form, then a new day in life's
Cycle is reborn.

Chapter 19

Time

Time, seems to wait for no one, as life
Moves eternally at the blink of every
Soul's eye and the beating of every living
Spirit's heart, the triangle of time, entities
Revolving in a world where life expires
Indefinitely within time.

Time

Revolving indefinitely amongst life,
Everywhere and nowhere,
Infinite, unending.

The Triangle of Time

As my heart beats, time ticks away
Slowly, each time the sun rises and sets
Over the horizon, time ticks away surely,
With each breath of fresh air I take, is a
Breath of fresh air expiring away, every
Tick of the clock, is a tick and a tock,
Bringing my life closer to a final stop,
Every wink of the eye, is a tear shed at
The end of my time, every warm feeling
That runs through my body, will eventually
Be a cold ending as I am born dying, and as
Time continues to keep moving, waiting for
No man, woman, or child, perhaps my life's
Existence is ever flowing in the triangle
Of time.

Guess

A clock ticks,
Arms of gold,
The perfect circle.

Away

As I watch each day go by, I reminisce
Upon the wonderful times shared between
You and I, now I ponder in deep thought, as I
Wish and anticipate our beings connecting
As one, a pleasant dream turned into
Reality, each day and night I contemplate,
As the clairvoyance of your presence
Turns pain to joy, darkness to sunshine, and
Misty clouds to clear blue skies, allowing
My spirit to yearn for warmth of each and
Every moment spent that I awake thinking
Of you, if fate is destiny then I never again
In life, wanna be away from you.

Present

The present, presents a new moment,
The present will surely pass in time,
That fast, the present has gone.

Past

The past was once the present,
The past was once the future,
Now the past, has passed.

To Reach You

To reach you, I would travel upon the
Desert's sand inside the hour glass of
Time, to reach you, I would transform my
Physical form into a bottle and
Formulate a message of divine love, to
Reach you, I would ride upon the spread
Wings of a soaring eagle flying amongst
The infinite blue skies, to reach you, I
Would journey upon the eternity of the
Deepest sea, just to reach you, I would
Dream a dream into reality, to reach you, I
Would overcome all obstacles, trials,
Tribulations and adversities, just to reach
You, to reach you I would give my heart
And soul, because I know the meaning of
Unconditional love.

Time and Time Again

Time and time again, I have felt my soul
Becoming the quicksand trapped within,
Time and time again, I have been captured
In the hour glass of time searching for
Freedom, time and time again, I have fallen
To struggles and adversities, but have
Found strength to rise up again upon my
Feet, time and time again, my thoughts
Have battled with my emotions and
Feelings, time and time again, good has
Fought against evil in my heart, time and
Time again, therefore I search for peace
And tranquility each day the sun peeks
Over the horizon, time and time again.

In Peace

Give me a dream that one day will be
Come true, show me a today that will
Surely present a better tomorrow,
Provide me with a life of joy and happiness,
Deliver me love, so that I never have to
Experience sadness, open up my eyes to the
Truth, so that I will never become
Deceived by the lies, awaken me each day
At sunrise, and give me another day to
Breathe, and to see the sunset in life,
Extend me a dream that will one day
Become a reality, bless me into a kingdom
Where in the end, my soul can rest forever
In peace.

Soaring Through Time

Soaring through time, not in fear, but in
Complete harmony with nature and life,
My soul reaches for the sun, as my spirit
Sails within the mist, whispers of birds
Chirp, while waterfalls crash upon rocks
And the light from the sun shines upon
Earth, allowing the flowers to bloom
Underneath the infinite blue skies,
Changing the course of life, while
Capturing the clouds, and eluding the
Storms, each breath, one of fresh air and
One of replenishment, allows my spirit to
Soar through time.

Chapter 20

Nature

You are the air we breathe, you are the
Clouds, stars, sun, moon, and ocean's
Breeze, you are the earth, atmosphere,
Nature's creativity, you are the sunrise
And the sunset, you are the magical
Poetry that speaks from within, you are
Life, and I thank you.

Nature's Wind

Delicately approaching,
Leaves blowing,
Serene element.

Thanks to You

It has been you, who have watched over
Me all the years of my life, it was you,
Who guided me and turned darkness to
Light, it was you, who protected me and
Showed me right from wrong and it will
Be you, whom I shall always believe in, for
You I will always remain strong, it was
You, who allowed me to rise for yet
Another exclusive day and with you I hope
My heart and soul will forever take, with
You, I cannot lose, rather in struggle or in
Pain, I understand that it was you, who have
Given me the strength to survive, granted
Me wisdom and insight, and opened up my
Eyes, and with you, if I am ever weak you
Will show me the way, with you I believe in
With all my divine faith, and I thank
You.

Gentle Winds

Blowing softly, amongst trees,
Breezing quietly, throughout life,
Resting calmly.

The Eye Watches

As the sky celebrates a new sunset upon
The horizon, the breeze blows quietly in
The wind, lifting up thy hands to you, as I
Reach for you, while on my knees staring
Into the clouds of you, from out of the
Windows of thy soul's inner being, viewing
Indefinitely the creations of life, from
Past and present experiences lived, then
Reminiscing of youthful days lived, times
Now I live in, for I have grown wise but old,
As thy spirit begins to prepare a new
Tomorrow, beginning with you, never
Again questioning you, as I have been
Touched by your ghost, understanding now
That nothing lasts forever, only thy
Deeds, thy seeds, and your words of wisdom
In the spirit of the beholder, as I am fully
Aware that the eye watches, from up
Above.

Pine Tree

The aroma of scented pine trees,
A breath of life,
Nature's greetings.

Up Above

Up above it is you who towers over thee,
And cures thy confusion with faith, your
Magical poetry, which speaks to the
World through my soul, as I am your poet
And I now see you in thee, revealing the
Truth, as I am your soldier and without
You and poetry I never could have made it
On my own, nor fought as I expire within
Time, versus sin, against darkness, the
Forces that challenges thy life, and pulls
Like a magnet, up above are where your
Powers lay, and deep within as I still
Believe although I have never seen
Physically, I know without a doubt
Spiritually, that you carry me, as I could
Have only been created and designed in
The image of the skies, up above.

Seasons

The four seasons of life,
All revolving within life,
Nature's infinite voice.

The Eye

The eye that watches, is the eye that
Leads me closer to you on thy journey, I
Know that you are thee, shining brightly
Upon thy soul, with your radiant energy,
Thy guiding light at the end of life's
Darkest road, thy spirit's inner strength,
Completing and reassuring, versus all
Obstacles and adversities that can
Possibly be and within, what would I do
Without your love, therefore I know that
I must follow in your footsteps, the eye,
The beginning and never ending of your
Eternal footprints, believing that you
Will hold my hand in spirit, as we walk
Together throughout life, this is what I
Live by, as we shall rest together as one,
When I finally reach your home, all by
Your design, which you have taught, from
The eye in the sky.

Oasis

The soft white sands,
Burning hot rocks,
A desert's mirage.

The Prayer

You have given me strength, when I
Thought I couldn't endure life anymore,
You have wiped my tears dry with your
Love, comfort, and affection, when I was
Covered by clouds drowning in pain, you
Have sheltered my spirit from the storms
And pouring rain, then you have allowed
Me to prosper against all obstacles and
Struggles, then kept my soul warm, when
My soul had turned cold, you have made
Me believe and have faith when I was lost,
You guided my way, thus to you, this
Prayer I pray.

Chapter 21

Magical Poetry

Magical poetry keeps the spirit alive,
And is the voice of love, and life in ever
Flowing motion.

Magical Poetry

Life's silent thoughts,
Laid to rest,
Upon paper.

Poetic Magic

As emotions empower the warmth of
Mystical romance and love exchanges
Thoughts and intimate feelings, poetic
Magic is created, when two loving spirits
Entwine in solidarity, unraveling love at
Its highest degree, poetic magic is formed,
When lights fill the atmosphere, while
The mercy of love becomes the engraving
Irony of a romantic love story, that
Becomes poetic magic composed, then the
Promotion and creation allows the
Manifestation of an epiphany, unraveling
Poetic magic in harmony, that is magical
Poetry, which makes poetic magic the
Certified and elite recipe, of you and I,
Living in love for all eternity.

Reflections

The you, within you,
The eye, within I,
Who you are.

Dreamer

I am a dreamer, in search of reality, but
Within my dreams I shall live for an
Eternity, I am a dreamer, strong, yet
Humble in spirit, living amongst my dreams
As a soul survivor of the present, I am a
Dreamer and builder of the future, leader
Of the necessary, balancing justice and
Equality, I am a dreamer, a master
Articulator of magical poetry, dreaming
Day in and day out as I live against all
Trials and adversities, I am a dreamer, with
Hopes and dreams of joy, to be forever
Loved and possess happiness, I am a
Dreamer, striving toward prosperity, so as
I dream, promise to never wake me, unless
My dreams of a better tomorrow have
Allowed my soul to reach its destiny and I
Have become one with my dreams now
Living in reality, I am a dreamer.

Yesterday

Yesterday, has already come,
Yesterday, has passed and gone,
Yesterday, has delivered today.

Magical Potion

The essence of our fantasies allows our
Love to be identified by our climax,
Explosive beyond measure, making a
Pathway for our souls to illuminate
Romanticism and emotion, inspiring a
Pleasurable interaction between you and
I, all in poetic motion, intimately
Disguised, but sufficiently fulfilled
Within the depths of our physical desires,
Love's magical potion, a state where love
Begins, and forever flows like the waves
Of an infinite ocean, created in the heart
And soul where romance is aquatinted with
Love's magical potion.

Presence

The gift of existence,
An everlasting vibe,
Always to be remembered.

There Could Be

There could be, no ocean without the
Sea, there could be, no mountains, without
A peak and no air, without the flowers and
Trees, there could be, no destination,
Without a determination to reach, there
Could be, no will to survive, without a
Desire to live and stay alive, there could
Be, no sun, without a sunrise and no sunset
Without the beginning of night time, there
Could be, no poem, without poetry, and no
Poetic soul, without your gift and
Blessings, there could be, no joy, without
Pain and no fire, without a flame, there
Could be, no love, without the hate and no
Balance without fate, there could be, no
Me, without you and no us, without two,
There could be, no clouds, without the sky
And no seeds of eternity, if it wasn't you
And I, there could be, no light, without
Darkness and no struggle, without
Perseverance, there could be, no wrong,
Without right, there could be, no
Strength, without, fight, there could be,
No destiny, without prosperity and no
Future, without eternity, there could be,
No life, without death and no peace,
Without rest, there could be.

The Orchard of Light

The emblem of morning summons earth
And life, all in silent thought and the
Beauty of nature's authentic channels,
Unfolds through a kaleidoscope viewed
From the windows of the soul, perhaps this
Quantum clairvoyance, captures the
Orchard of light, in countless
Collections of vast presentations,
Shining eternally, as the orchard of
Light reflects life from within the
Harvest of my entity, the orchard of
Light, a spiritual glow, a vintage portrait,
Life's magnetic soul.

Never Ending Story

My soul has swam from the bottom of
The ocean's floor, to reach the top of the
Infinite sea, yet rain drops continue to
Pour upon me, as the constant waves of
Life, continue to provoke insanity within
Me, splashing the water of my tears,
Against life's mountains of obstacles and
Adversities, my tears have become the
Salt, and my flesh the sea, all in this never
Ending, life story.

The Never-Ending End

About the Poet

Cleveland K. Kincade is a poetic soul, philanthropist, humanitarian, and the author of the literary works of *The Anthology of Magical Poetry, Volume I*, as well as the soon-to-be released urban novel *The Poet*. He is also the founder and C.E.O. of Kincade Publishing Company, the Kincade Company Poetic Wear Clothing line, and the c/o Founder and C.E.O. of Kincade Cares, a non-profit organization designed to provide charitable and literary education to the under privileged and at-risk youths in the community, and in third-world countries across the globe.

Cleveland K. Kincade is also a member of the California State Poetry Society, the Haiku Society of America, and the American Poets Society. He resides in Oceanside, California, with his wife Kalia, daughter Knijah-Ayana, and son Cleveland-Kanye Kincade, where they enjoy boogie boarding, roller skating, and enjoyable family walks on the hot sands of the sunny southern California shores.

Coming soon: *The Poet*

The Poet by Cleveland K. Kincade, and
Kincade Publishing Company deliver to you the
reader a provocative and riveting narrative,
based on a young Poetic Soul's lifetime struggle
to transcend severe poverty, the ultimate trials
and tribulations of life, and insurmountable
adversities to become one of the world's most
commanding businessmen, urban publishers in
the industry, and cultural entrepreneurs in the
corporate world.

This urban novel, although fiction, is a deeply
moving masterpiece that will provide the spirit
with messages of hope and inspiration for
society and the youth, all struggling in harmony
to find themselves and build a pathway in life
toward prosperity and success. *The Poet* also
possesses an emotionally touching love story
entwined, which is brimming with suspense,
poignancy, and a dramatic climax.

After being faced with the loss of several family
members, his own freedom, and several
attempts by life's many unseen forces from
birth, to destroy the poet's life and alter his
mission and destiny, while also trying to destroy
him in the mental, spiritual, and physical form,
life presents the poet with one last and final
opportunity to overcome the challenges and
obstacles that have been placed before him, and
make a better way of life for himself and his

family, which eventually compels the poet to make a relentless moral comeback in life to rise again and fulfill the destiny that was written in his soul, as he becomes a business man, and worldwide symbol of hope and inspiration known as the poet.

Magical poetry keeps the spirit alive,
And is the voice of love, and life
In ever flowing motion.

Poetry Questionnaire

1. Do the titles of the poems help reveal the theme and reflect the topics of the poems? (yes or no)

2. What was your first reaction after reading the poems? (a) touching (b) soothing (c) spiritually stimulating (d) none of the above

3. What qualities about the poems do you admire most? (a) the title (b) the poems overall (c) the poetic flow (d) none of the above

4. What thoughts or feelings were you left with after reading the poems? Please explain.

   _____

5. Has reading the poems changed your view of or feelings about magical poetry? (yes or no)

6. On a scale of 1 to 10, where would you place the poems? (1 – 2 – 3 – 4 – 5 – 6 – 7 – 8 – 9 - 10).

7. How would you rate the poems? (a) classical (b) comprehensive (c) intellectual (d) none of the above

8. Do the poems influence or affect the way you view the author / poet of the book? (yes or no)

9. What emotions, feelings, or thoughts do the poems awaken in you? Please explain.

   _____

10. How would you respond if the author / poet recited the poems in spoken word directly to you? Please explain.

Thank you for participating in this poetry questionnaire.
Your worthy input as a poetry reader
will be taken into great consideration.

Available now

- *The Anthology of Magical Poetry, Volume I* (novel) by Cleveland K. Kincade

- The Kincade Company: poetic wear clothing

- Kincade Cares: not-for-profit organization

- Poetic greeting cards: Kincade Publishing

- Poetic records: Magical Poetry CDs & DVDs

Coming to you soon

- *The Poet* (novel) by Cleveland K. Kincade Kincade Publishing Company

- The Poetic Soul's magazine / newsletter

- *Magical Poetry Written in Stone Volume II* (novel) by Cleveland K. Kincade

- (K)-Electronics: reading with magical poetry (educational software - CD / DVD - children's books)

- *Magical Poetry in Motion Volume III* (novel) by Cleveland K. Kincade

- "A Poetic Soul" movie script / screenplay by Cleveland K. Kincade

- *Magical Poetry The Final Chapter Volume IV* (novel) by Cleveland K. Kincade

- The Poetic Soul's Lounge: poetry / coffee house

If you wish to order or learn more about any of the items on the preceding page, please complete this form and send to:

Kincade Publishing Company
K. Kincade
PO Box 635
San Luis Rey, CA 92068

I am interested in ❏ ordering ❏ learning more about:

_____

_____

_____

Name
_____
(please print)

Address
_____

City
_____

State and Zip
_____

Phone or Cell
_____

E-mail
_____

www.ingramcontent.com/pod-product-compliance
Lightning Source LLC
Chambersburg PA
CBHW060013100426
42740CB00010B/1470